orac
OF THE
CROW

MESSAGES FROM THE REALMS

Welcome to the mystical world of the Crow's Oracle, where the enigmatic crow serves as a messenger between the realms to bring you guidance and insight.

In these 48 oracles, you will discover the wisdom and messages that crows carry from the various dimensions beyond our earthly existence. Each page reveals a unique message, offering you a glimpse into the secrets of the universe so that you can gain clarity on how to better navigate your life's journey.

RUDI DE PONTE
DIMITRI KALOGEROPOULOS

KDP
TRANSFORMATION
IN PROGRESS

oracle
OF THE
CROW

MESSAGES FROM THE REALMS

———————————▶●◀———————————

All rights reserved. No part of this publication may be reproduced, stored in a retrieval system or transmitted in any form or by any means, electronic, mechanical, photocopying or otherwise, without the prior permission of the copyright owner.

All rights reserved.

No part of this book may be reproduced or transmitted in any form or by any means, electronic or mechanical, including photocopying, recording, or by any information storage or retrieval system, without permission in writing from the Publisher.

Publisher: KalosDePonte Publishing

KDP
TRANSFORMATION
IN PROGRESS

Any unauthorized use, sharing, reproduction, or distribution of these materials by any means, electronic, mechanical, or otherwise is strictly prohibited. No portion of these materials may be reproduced in any manner whatsoever, without the express written consent of the publisher.

WAIVER: The author of this book does not dispense medical advice or other professional advice or prescribe the use of any technique as a form of diagnosis or treatment for any physical, emotional, or medical condition. The intent of the author is only to offer information of an anecdotal and general nature that may be part of your quest for emotional and spiritual wellbeing. In the event you or others use any of the information or other content in this book, the author and the publisher assume no responsibility for the direct or indirect consequences. The reader should consult his or her medical, health, or other professional before adopting any of the suggestions in this book or drawing inferences from it.

PREFACE

Welcome to the mystical world of the Crow's Oracle, a realm where the enigmatic crow transcends its earthly form to become a symbol of wisdom, messenger, and guide between the realms. Within the pages of this 48-page oracle book, you are invited to embark on a transformative journey, delving into the profound wisdom and messages that crows carry from the dimensions beyond our ordinary existence.

The crow, revered in various cultures throughout history, holds a unique place in the tapestry of human spirituality. Often seen as a symbol of mystery, intuition, and the ability to traverse the boundaries between the seen and the unseen, the crow serves as a beacon of guidance in this oracle. Its presence beckons us to look beyond the mundane and connect with the cosmic and the mystical.

Each page of this oracle book unveils a unique message from the crow, offering you a glimpse into the hidden secrets of the universe. These messages are not mere words; they are keys to unlocking the profound wisdom that resides within you. As you turn the pages, you will find inspiration, clarity, and insight to help you navigate the intricate paths of your life's journey.

The crow's messages are both timeless and timely, resonating with the ancient wisdom that has guided seekers and sages throughout the ages. They provide a bridge between the practicalities of daily life and the mysteries of the cosmos, inviting you to find meaning in the dance between the ordinary and the extraordinary.

As you explore the pages of the Crow's Oracle, remember that you are not alone on this journey. The crow, as your eternal guide and messenger, will accompany you every step of the way. Its wisdom will serve as a lantern in the darkness, a compass in the wilderness, and a friend in moments of uncertainty.

May this oracle book be a source of inspiration, reflection, and empowerment. May it guide you to embrace change, find clarity, and awaken your inner wisdom. Welcome to the mystical world of the Crow's Oracle, where the crow's call echoes through the dimensions to lead you to the deeper truths that lie within and beyond.

INTRODUCTION

Welcome to the mystical world of the Crow's Oracle, a sacred realm where the enigmatic crow takes flight as a messenger between the earthly and the spiritual dimensions, offering us profound guidance and timeless insights. In this 48-page oracle book, we embark on a journey of discovery, delving into the wisdom and messages that crows carry from the hidden realms beyond our earthly existence.

With each turn of the page, you will be drawn deeper into the secrets of the universe, gaining clarity and illumination that will empower you to navigate the intricate pathways of your life's journey.

The crow, with its captivating presence and symbolic significance across cultures and generations, serves as an emblem of mysticism and cosmic awareness. Within its wings lies the power to bridge the gap between the seen and the unseen, to traverse the realms beyond the ordinary, and to reveal the profound truths that often elude our conscious perception. As we unlock the pages of this oracle book, we unlock the door to these timeless mysteries.

Within these pages, you will discover a unique message on each page, that holds the potential to touch your heart, stir your spirit, and awaken your inner wisdom. These messages are gifts from the crow, carefully selected to provide you with the clarity, insight, and inspiration you seek on your life's journey. Each message is a piece of the cosmic puzzle, a note in the symphony of existence, and a guiding star in the tapestry of your spiritual awakening.

As you embrace the wisdom of the Crow's Oracle, you will find that it is not merely a book but a portal to the mystical dimensions that surround us. The crow invites you to join in its sacred dance, to listen closely to its caw, and to embark on a journey of transformation, illumination, and self-discovery. With each message, you will step closer to the heart of the cosmos, gaining a deeper understanding of the interconnectedness of all things.

So, dear reader, prepare to embark on a journey like no other. The Crow's Oracle beckons you to open your heart and mind to the wisdom that transcends time and space. With each message, you will find a piece of the universe's grand design, a key to unlocking your true potential, and a guiding light to lead you through the labyrinth of existence. Welcome to the mystical world of the Crow's Oracle; may your journey be filled with wonder, enlightenment, and the eternal wisdom of the crow.

Yours truly,

Rudi de Ponte and Dimitrios Kalogeropoulos

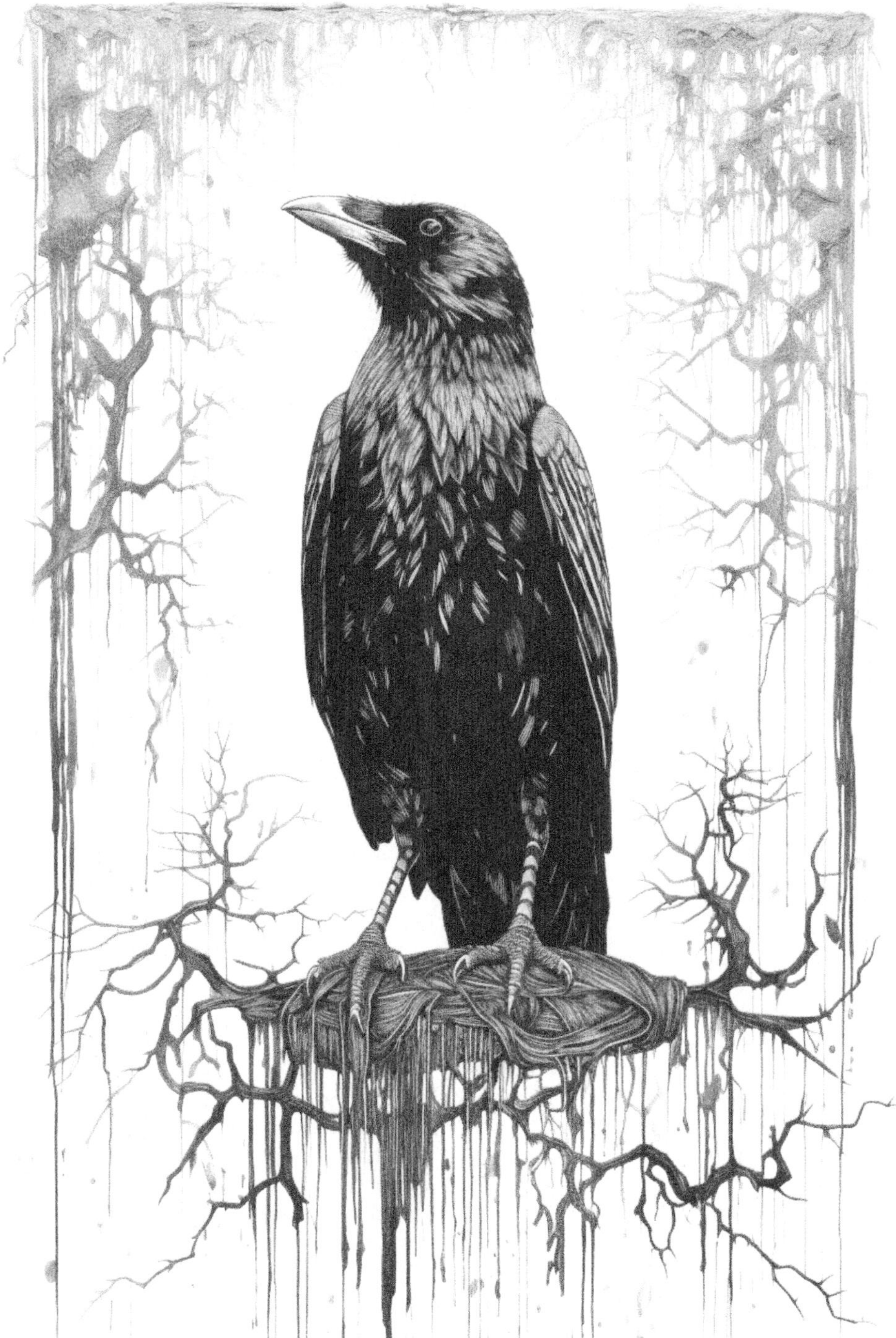

MESSAGE SELECTOR

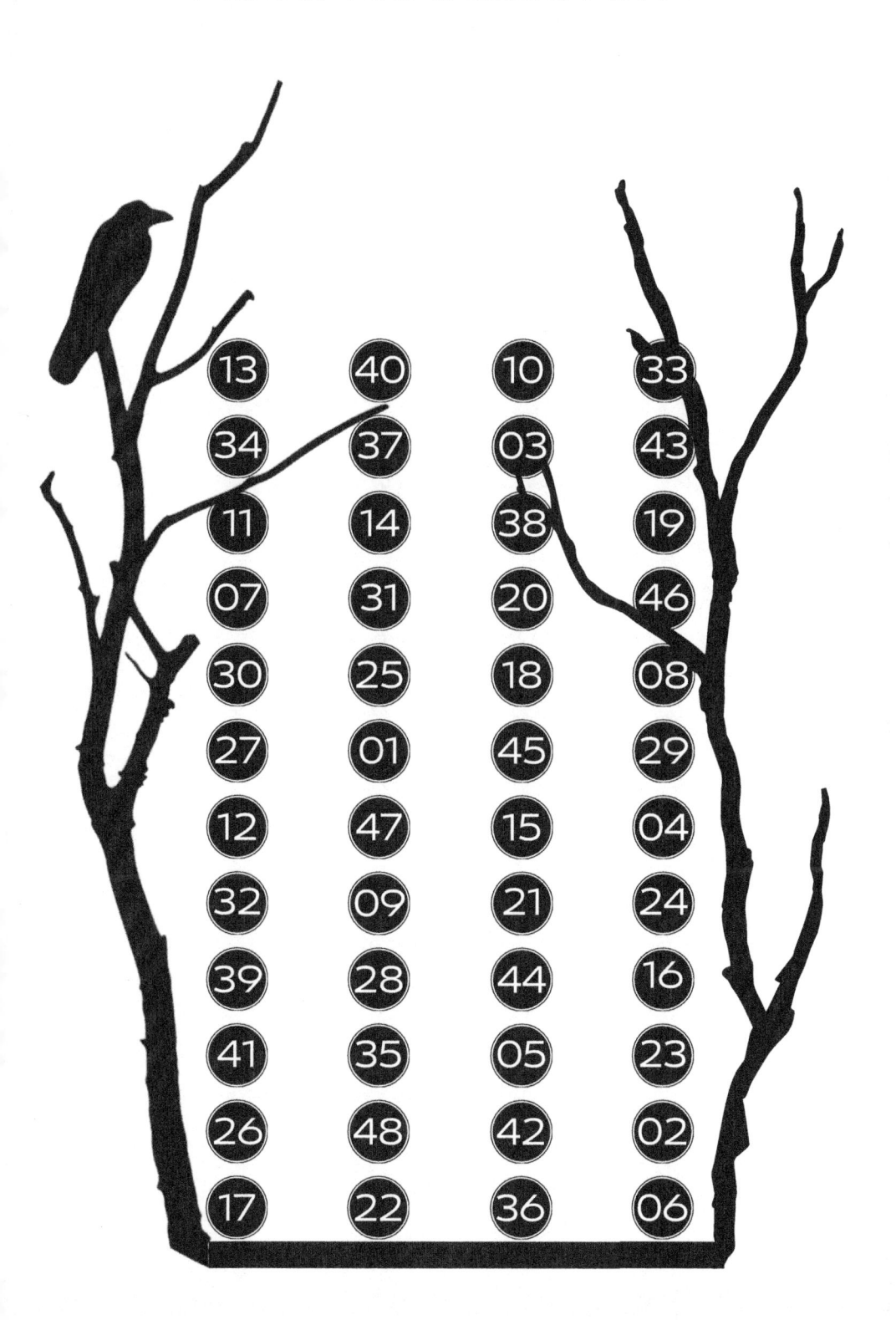

INDEX

1 - The Crows Awakening
2 - The Crows Call
3 - The Realm of Dreams
4 - The Observer
5 - The Mirror Effect
6 - The Messengers Gift
7 - The Language of Symbols
8 - Adaptation
9 - The Crows Guidance
10 - The Veil of Illusion
11 - Transformation
12 - The Crows Dance
13 - Intuition
14 - Ancestral Connections
15 - The Mystic Path
16 - Synchronicity
17 - Embracing Darkness
18 - The Keeper of Secrets
19 - Flight of Freedom
20 - The Circle of Life
21 - The Crows Laughter
22 - Mystical Connections
23 - Divine Timing
24 - Inner Alchemy

INDEX

25	-	The Hidden Path
26	-	The Crows Council
27	-	The Threshold
28	-	The Crows Feather
29	-	The Wisdom of Silence
30	-	The Guardian
31	-	The Crows Eye
32	-	The Elemental Connection
33	-	The Interconnected Web
34	-	The Cosmic Whispers
35	-	The Sacred Offering
36	-	The Crows Flight
37	-	The Keeper of Balance
38	-	The Cycle of Rebirth
39	-	The Cosmic Connection
40	-	The Crows Guidance
41	-	The Sacred Dance
42	-	The Veil of Illusion
43	-	The Eternal Messenger
44	-	The Crows Blessing
45	-	The Closing of the Circle
46	-	The Crows Farewell
47	-	Acknowledgments
48	-	Completion

1
THE CROW'S AWAKENING

*LISTEN TO YOUR INTUITION, ITS TIME TO WAKE UP
THE CROW IS CALLING*

MESSAGE:

THE CROW CALLS YOU TO AWAKEN YOUR INNER WISDOM. EMBRACE CHANGE, AS A NEW DAWN APPROACHES.

TRANSFORM WITH THE CROWS CALL BY TAPPING INTO YOUR AWAKENING PROCESS.
USE YOUR INNER TOOLS TO GET STARTED.

The "Awakening" message within the Crow Oracle carries a potent and invigorating message, calling us to heed the crow's call and embark on a transformative journey of self-discovery and change.

Crows, with their enigmatic presence and associations with awakening, symbolize the breaking of dawn, the emergence of new possibilities, and the unveiling of inner wisdom. The "Awakening" message prompts us to recognize that a profound shift is on the horizon, much like the breaking of a new day.

This message encourages us to embrace the process of change and transformation, much like the crow's ability to adapt to diverse environments. It reminds us that change is not to be feared but welcomed as an opportunity for growth, evolution, and the emergence of our inner wisdom.

"The Awakening" message suggests that the crow's call is a beckoning to our higher selves, a reminder to listen to our intuition and inner guidance. It encourages us to embark on a journey of self-discovery, shedding old patterns and beliefs to reveal the innate wisdom that resides within.

Furthermore, this message underscores the idea that, like the crow's flight at dawn, we are on the cusp of something new and profound. It invites us to approach this awakening with open hearts and minds, ready to embrace the mysteries and opportunities that lie ahead.

In summary, the "Awakening" message is a powerful call to action, urging us to heed the crow's call and awaken our inner wisdom. It inspires us to embrace change as a harbinger of new beginnings, much like the breaking of dawn. By doing so, we can navigate life with a sense of anticipation, transformation, and a deep connection to our inner selves.

2
THE CROW'S CALL

WHEN THE CROW CAWS PAY ATTENTION, A MESSAGE IS REVEALED IN YOUR SURROUNDINGS

MESSAGE:

LISTEN CLOSELY TO THE CROW'S CAW, FOR IT CARRIES ECHOES FROM OTHER WORLDS, INVITING YOU TO PAY ATTENTION TO YOUR SURROUNDINGS.

WHEN YOU NOTICE A CROWS CALL, PAY ATTENTION TO YOUR ENVIRONMENT FOR THERE IS A MESSAGE FOR YOU.

The Crow's Call" is a powerful message within the Crow Oracle, it encourages us to be attentive to the world around us and to listen deeply, not just with our ears but with our hearts and intuition.

Crows have long been associated with transcendence and transformation in various cultures and spiritual traditions. They are seen as messengers that bridge the gap between our physical world and the spiritual realms. When we hear the Crow's distinctive caw, it is believed to carry echoes from these otherworldly dimensions.

To heed "The Crow's Call" is to become attuned to the subtle energies and hidden meanings in our everyday lives. Crows are known for their acute intelligence and their ability to solve complex problems, making them natural observers of the world. They can detect changes in their environment that often go unnoticed by others. Similarly, when we pay attention to the Crow's call, we are encouraged to sharpen our awareness and embrace a heightened state of consciousness.

This message also emphasizes the importance of being present in the moment. Just as the Crow remains fully engaged with its surroundings, we are prompted to immerse ourselves in the here and now. By doing so, we open ourselves to the possibility of receiving valuable insights and guidance from the universe.

Furthermore, "The Crow's Call" invites us to explore the concept of synchronicity. It suggests that there is a deeper connection between the Crow's caw and the events unfolding in our lives. When we start noticing these meaningful coincidences, we are encouraged to trust the path we are on and to understand that there is a greater design at work.

By listening closely to the Crow's caw, we become participants in a cosmic conversation, receiving invitations to explore the depths of our existence and to pay attention to the intricate details of our journey. This message teaches us to embrace the Crow as a mystical guide and messenger, helping us navigate the realms of both the seen and the unseen.

3
THE REALM OF DREAMS

SEEING CROWS IN YOUR DREAMS SYMBOLISES YOUR CLOSE CONNECTION TO OTHER REALMS

MESSAGE:

WHEN YOU DREAM OF A CROW, TAKE HEED, FOR YOUR SUBCONSCIOUS IS SENDING MESSAGES FROM BEYOND.

AFFIRMATION TO CONNECT WITH THE CROW IN YOUR DREAM STATE: "CROW, AS I LAY MY HEAD TO REST, PLEASE COME TO ME AS YOU LEAVE YOUR NEST, FOR IN THE DARK YOUR LIGHT SHINES THROUGH, SO FLY TO ME MY HEART IS TRUE"

"The Realm of Dreams" message in the Crow Oracle carries a profound significance, underscoring the mystical connection between dreams and our inner world. When a crow appears in your dream, it serves as a powerful symbol that invites you to pay close attention to the messages emanating from your subconscious mind.

Dreams are often regarded as windows into the inner workings of our psyche. They can offer insights, revelations, and guidance that might elude us in our waking hours. The appearance of a crow within the dream realm is a clear signal that your inner self is trying to communicate with you, bringing forth messages from the depths of your subconscious.

Crows have long held mystical and symbolic significance in various cultures. They are often associated with wisdom, transformation, and the mysteries of life and death. When a crow enters your dreamscape, it is as though a wise and ancient guardian is beckoning you to take heed of the wisdom it carries.

This message emphasizes the importance of dream interpretation and reflection. When you dream of a crow, it's an invitation to delve into the symbolic language of your dreamscape. Consider the context of the dream, the emotions it evoked, and the specific actions or interactions involving the crow. These elements can offer valuable insights into your inner world, fears, desires, and unresolved issues.

Moreover, "The Realm of Dreams" message encourages you to trust your intuitive faculties. Crows are known for their keen perception and intuitive nature. When a crow appears in your dream, it suggests that you should rely on your own intuition and inner guidance to navigate the waking world. The crow's presence is a reminder that your inner wisdom is a powerful compass.

4
THE OBSERVER

WITNESS WITHOUT ENGAGEMENT, AND YOU'LL DISCERN THE UNMISTAKABLE MESSAGES APPROACHING YOUR PATH.

MESSAGE:

EMBRACE KEEN OBSERVATION, AKIN TO THE CROW'S WATCHFUL PERCH ABOVE. IN PATIENCE, THE WORLD UNVEILS ITS HIDDEN SECRETS TO THOSE WHO WAIT.

TAKE STEPS TOWARDS BECOMING THE OBSERVER, THIS REQUIRES PATIENCE AND PRACTICE.

The message of "The Observer" within the Crow Oracle speaks to the importance of cultivating patience and keen observation in our lives. It draws a parallel between our role as observers and the natural behavior of crows, which are known for their watchful and patient nature.

Crows are often seen perched high above, surveying their surroundings with a discerning eye. They patiently wait, observing the world from a unique vantage point. In this context, "The Observer" encourages us to adopt a similar approach in our daily lives. By being attentive, patient, and observant, we can gain deeper insights into the world around us.

The message underscores the idea that the world is full of hidden secrets and subtle nuances that may go unnoticed by those who rush through life. Just as crows patiently await opportunities and observe their environment, we too can benefit from taking a step back, slowing down, and paying closer attention to the intricacies of our surroundings.

Being observant is not merely about seeing with our eyes; it involves engaging all our senses and tapping into our intuition. When we adopt the role of "The Observer," we become more attuned to the energies, patterns, and rhythms of the world. This heightened awareness can lead to a deeper understanding of ourselves and our place within the grand tapestry of existence.

Furthermore, the message suggests that patience is a key virtue in our journey of self-discovery and in unraveling the mysteries of life. The world may not always reveal its secrets readily; they often emerge when we approach it with patience and an open heart. Just as the crow's watchful gaze eventually yields valuable insights, our patient observation can lead to profound discoveries and personal growth.

5
THE MIRROR EFFECT

GO WITHIN IN AND REVEAL YOUR MIRROR EFFECT TO THE WORLD - AS WITHIN SO WITHOUT

MESSAGE:

JUST AS THE CROW MIRRORS THE SKY, REFLECT ON YOUR INNER SELF, FOR IT HOLDS THE ANSWERS YOU SEEK.

MIRROR, MIRROR ON THE WALL, IMPART THE WISDOM OF PATIENCE AND KEEN OBSERVATION, UNVEIL YOUR SACRED TEACHINGS TODAY.

The message of "The Mirror Effect" within the Crow Oracle encourages us to embark on a journey of introspection and self-reflection by drawing a compelling parallel between the crow and our inner selves.

Crows, with their dark feathers and enigmatic presence, are often associated with symbolism related to reflection and mirroring. When a crow takes flight against the vast canvas of the sky, it appears as a reflection of the heavens themselves. In this context, "The Mirror Effect" invites us to consider the profound notion that our inner selves, like the crow, possess the capacity to reflect our deepest truths and desires.

This message urges us to turn our attention inward and explore the depths of our inner world. Just as the crow mirrors the sky, we are encouraged to examine our thoughts, emotions, and beliefs, as they can serve as mirrors that reveal our true nature. By doing so, we may uncover hidden aspects of ourselves, our strengths, our weaknesses, and our latent potential.

"The Mirror Effect" also emphasizes that the answers to our most pressing questions and challenges often reside within us. In our quest for understanding and clarity, we may seek external guidance or validation, but this message reminds us that our inner self is a vast reservoir of wisdom. When we take the time to reflect and connect with our inner essence, we can tap into this wellspring of insight.

Furthermore, the message underscores the importance of authenticity. Just as the crow reflects the sky in its true form, embracing our inner selves allows us to live authentically and in alignment with our core values and desires. It encourages us to embrace our uniqueness and to be true to ourselves, regardless of external influences or pressures.

6
THE MESSENGERS GIFT

EMBRACE THE LIFE-ALTERING GIFTS WITH GRATITUDE, SHEDDING UNWORTHINESS TO UNBLOCK YOUR PATH.

MESSAGE:

THE CROW BRINGS GIFTS FROM OTHER REALMS. ACCEPT THEM WITH GRATITUDE, FOR THEY HOLD HIDDEN BLESSINGS.

ALLOW FOR THE GIFT FROM THE CROW TO FLOW INTO YOUR LIFE, YOU DESERVE IT, BELIEVE IT.

"The Messenger's Gift" within the Crow Oracle imparts a profound lesson about the symbolic significance of crows as messengers and the blessings they bring from realms beyond our everyday perception.

When a crow presents us with a gift, it's a symbolic gesture that invites us to acknowledge the unseen forces at play in our lives. These gifts, whether tangible or symbolic, carry hidden blessings and insights from the realms beyond.

The message encourages us to accept these gifts with gratitude and an open heart. Just as the crow offers its blessings, it is a reminder for us to receive the messages and experiences that come our way with appreciation and mindfulness. These gifts may not always be immediately apparent in their significance, but they often hold the potential to enrich our lives and guide us on our path.

In essence, "The Messenger's Gift" invites us to cultivate a sense of receptivity and awareness in our daily lives. It reminds us that there is a deeper purpose and meaning to the events and encounters we experience. By accepting these gifts with gratitude, we open ourselves to the possibility of discovering hidden blessings and profound wisdom in the seemingly ordinary aspects of life.

Moreover, the message encourages us to trust in the guidance and messages from the spiritual or mystical realms. When we encounter a crow or its symbolic gift, it is a sign that we are being watched over and guided by forces beyond the visible world. This guidance may come in the form of synchronicities, intuitive insights, or unexpected opportunities.

By accepting these gifts with gratitude and a sense of wonder, we invite hidden blessings to unfold, leading us on a path of greater understanding, insight, and spiritual growth.

7
THE LANGUAGE OF SYMBOLS

SYMBOLS ARE POWERFUL MESSAGES THAT CROWS BRING INTO OUR LIVES

MESSAGE:

LEARN TO DECODE THE SYMBOLS IN YOUR LIFE, FOR THE CROW'S MESSAGES OFTEN COME IN MYSTERIOUS FORMS.

SYMBOLS ARE EVERYWHERE, TAKE TIME TO EXPLORE AND UNDERSTAND HOW THE CROW PRESENTS SYMBOLS TO GUIDE YOU IN YOUR LIFE

"The Language of Symbols" message within the Crow Oracle imparts a profound lesson about the significance of symbolism in our lives and the cryptic ways in which the messages of crows are often delivered.

Crows are believed to communicate through a language of symbols and signs, and their messages are not always straightforward. In this context, "The Language of Symbols" invites us to become more attuned to the symbols and signs that populate our own lives.

This message encourages us to be mindful of the symbolism that surrounds us daily. Symbols can manifest in various forms, such as dreams, synchronicities, animal encounters, or even in the patterns and events of our everyday existence. Much like the crow's messages, these symbols are often mysterious and cryptic, requiring us to delve deeper into their meanings.

Decoding these symbols offers us a unique opportunity for self-discovery and spiritual growth. It prompts us to explore the hidden layers of our consciousness and consider the underlying messages that these symbols carry. By learning the language of symbols, we gain access to a richer and more nuanced understanding of our experiences and our connection to the world.

Moreover, "The Language of Symbols" reminds us of the interconnectedness of all things. It suggests that the universe is constantly communicating with us through the language of symbols, inviting us to recognize the threads of meaning that weave through the fabric of existence. When we engage with these symbols, we align ourselves with a greater cosmic narrative that can guide us on our journey.

By learning to decode the symbols in our lives, we open ourselves to deeper levels of understanding and insight. We are encouraged to cultivate a sense of curiosity, wonder, and mindfulness in our daily experiences.

8
ADAPTATION

BECOME A SHAPESHIFTER TO BLEND IN ALL SITUATIONS

MESSAGE:

ADAPTING TO SITUATIONS AND ENVIRONMENTS IS A SUPER POWER WHICH THE CROW GIFTS YOU. CALL ON THE CROW TO HELP YOU ADAPT ANYTIME & ANY PLACE.

CALL ON THE CROW AND TAKE A DEEP BREATH, THEY WILL HELP YOU GAIN CONFIDENCE TO ADAPT.

The "Adaptation" message within the Crow Oracle imparts a valuable lesson drawn from the crow's remarkable ability to thrive in diverse environments. It encourages us to embrace change, resilience, and flexibility in our own lives, much like the crow.

Crows are highly adaptable birds, found in a wide range of habitats, from urban cities to remote wilderness areas. Their ability to adjust to different environments and conditions reflects their resourcefulness and resilience. Similarly, the "Adaptation" message calls upon us to cultivate these qualities.

Change is a constant in life, and our ability to adapt can significantly impact our well-being and success. When we resist change, we may experience stress, frustration, and stagnation. In contrast, when we follow the crow's example and embrace change with an open mind, we discover new opportunities for growth and transformation.

This message reminds us that adaptation is not about compromising our core values or identity but about evolving and expanding our capacities. Just as the crow retains its essential 'crowness' in different environments, we can remain true to ourselves while adapting to changing circumstances.

Moreover, the "Adaptation" message underscores the importance of resilience. Resilience is our capacity to bounce back from adversity and navigate life's challenges with grace and strength. The crow's ability to thrive despite varied conditions serves as a reminder that resilience is a valuable trait in our journey through life.

Embrace change and adapt to diverse environments and circumstances. By doing so, we can harness the power of resilience and flexibility, enabling us to thrive in the face of life's ever-shifting landscapes. Adaptation is a key to personal growth and empowerment, allowing us to spread our wings and soar even when the winds of change blow strongly.

9
THE CROW'S GUIDANCE

THE CROW'S GUIDANCE IS AVAILABLE FOR YOU TO CALL UPON WHEN YOU NEED EXTERNAL OR INTERNAL GUIDANCE

MESSAGE:

WHEN YOU'RE LOST, CALL UPON THE CROW TO BE YOUR INNER GPS, TO GUIDE YOU SAFELY TO WHERE YOU NEED TO BE.

LET THE SAGACIOUS CROW'S GUIDANCE PROPEL YOU IN THE RIGHT DIRECTION.

The "Crow's Guidance" message within the Crow Oracle is a beacon of hope and direction in times of uncertainty and confusion. It draws a powerful parallel between the crow's role as a guide and our need for guidance in life's intricate journey.

Crows are often seen as wise and intuitive birds, capable of navigating complex landscapes effortlessly. Their ability to soar high in the sky and survey their surroundings grants them a unique vantage point from which they can perceive hidden paths and opportunities. When we feel lost or adrift in life, the "Crow's Guidance" message encourages us to turn to the wisdom of these birds.

In moments of uncertainty, we are called upon to seek inner clarity and external guidance. The crow, as a symbol of guidance, reminds us that there is a higher perspective available to us. When we feel overwhelmed or disoriented, it is often helpful to take a step back, elevate our viewpoint, and look at our situation from a broader perspective. By doing so, we can gain insights that may have eluded us in our day-to-day existence.

This message also emphasizes the idea that guidance can come from unexpected sources and in mysterious ways. Much like the crow's messages, which often arrive in cryptic forms, guidance in our lives may not always be obvious or straightforward. It may manifest as subtle nudges, synchronicities, or intuitive hunches. Therefore, we are encouraged to be receptive and open to the signs and messages that the universe sends our way.

Moreover, the "Crow's Guidance" message invites us to trust in our ability to navigate life's challenges with grace and wisdom. It reassures us that, like the crow, we possess an inner compass that can guide us to our destination, even when the path seems uncertain.

By seeking guidance from the symbolic wisdom of the crow and being attuned to the signs and messages in our lives, we can navigate the complexities of existence with a sense of purpose and clarity.

10
THE VEIL OF ILLUSION

SEE BEYOND THE VEIL AND INTO OTHER REALMS

MESSAGE:

PIERCE THE VEIL OF ILLUSION AND SEE REALITY AS THE CROW DOES, WITH CLARITY AND WISDOM. LIVE YOUR TRUTH WITH CONFIDENCE AND CLARITY.

PEEL BACK THE CURTAINS AND REVEAL YOUR TRUTH. ALL THIS TIME YOU HAVE BEEN EXISTING, NOW IT IS TIME TO START LIVING.

"The Veil of Illusion" message within the Crow Oracle is a profound reminder of the importance of discernment and insight in our perception of reality. It draws a parallel between the crow's clarity of vision and our own quest for wisdom and truth.

Crows are renowned for their sharp and discerning eyesight, which allows them to perceive their surroundings with exceptional clarity. They can spot details and nuances that may elude other creatures. In this context, "The Veil of Illusion" urges us to emulate the crow's perspective by piercing through the illusionary layers that can cloud our understanding of the world.

Illusion, in this context, represents the distortions and misconceptions that can veil our perception of reality. These illusions may be self-imposed, societal, or cultural in nature. They can manifest as preconceived notions, biases, or limited perspectives that hinder our ability to see the world as it truly is.

This message encourages us to cultivate a sense of clarity and wisdom in our perception. To pierce the veil of illusion means to embark on a journey of self-awareness and insight, seeking to understand the world and ourselves with greater depth and authenticity. It prompts us to question assumptions, challenge conventional wisdom, and view reality through a more discerning lens.

Furthermore, "The Veil of Illusion" suggests that wisdom and clarity often emerge when we let go of attachments to superficiality and materialism. The crow, as a symbol of wisdom, reminds us that true understanding comes from looking beyond the surface and tapping into the deeper, hidden aspects of existence.

In essence, this message calls upon us to be mindful and present in our experiences. It invites us to engage in introspection and self-reflection to uncover the truth that lies beneath the layers of illusion. By doing so, we can navigate life with greater wisdom, make informed choices, and develop a deeper connection with the world around us.

11
TRANSFORMATION

EMBRACE YOUR NEW AND RELEASE YOUR OLD AS YOU TRANSFORM INTO A MAGICAL BEING

MESSAGE:

LIKE THE CROW, YOU TOO CAN TRANSFORM AND EVOLVE INTO A HIGHER VERSION OF YOURSELF. BELEIVE IT, FEEL IT AND LIVE IT.

EXPAND INTO TRUE YOU.
ITS TIME TO SHOW OFF YOUR WINGS.

The "Transformation" message within the Crow Oracle is a powerful reminder of the innate capacity for growth and change that resides within each of us. Drawing inspiration from the crow's symbolic significance of transformation, this message invites us to embrace the potential for personal evolution.

Crows are known for their remarkable ability to adapt and transform. They undergo various stages of growth, from hatchling to adult, and their distinctive plumage changes over time. Similarly, "Transformation" emphasizes that we, too, are on a journey of growth and self-improvement.

This message encourages us to view our lives as a continuous process of transformation. It reminds us that just as the crow evolves into a higher version of itself, we have the potential to shed old patterns, beliefs, and limitations to become the best versions of ourselves. This process involves self-reflection, self-awareness, and a willingness to embrace change.

Moreover, "Transformation" underscores the idea that personal growth often requires us to leave our comfort zones. The crow, as a symbol of transformation, inspires us to take flight into the unknown, to explore uncharted territories, and to be open to new experiences. It suggests that we can transcend our limitations and fears by harnessing our inner strength and courage.

In essence, this message instills hope and motivation. It reminds us that transformation is not only possible but an integral part of our human experience. It reassures us that we have the innate potential to rise above challenges, overcome obstacles, and evolve into higher versions of ourselves.

Furthermore, "Transformation" serves as a call to action. It encourages us to take deliberate steps toward self-improvement and personal growth. Just as the crow embraces its transformation with grace, we too can embark on a journey of self-discovery, self-empowerment, and self-transcendence.

12
THE CROW'S DANCE

SWAY TO THE RHYTHM OF LIFE

MESSAGE:

THE CROW REMINDS US TO MOVE GRACEFULLY BETWEEN THE REALMS OF EXISTENCE. WHEN YOU MOVE IN TIME WITH THE RHYTHM YOU REMAIN INTUNE AND IN ALIGNMENT.

WITH THE CROW'S ASSISTANCE, TUNE INTO THE UNIVERSE'S RHYTHM.

"The Crow's Dance" message within the Crow Oracle is a poetic reminder of the fluid and interconnected nature of life. This message draws a beautiful parallel between life's journey and a dance, with the crow as our graceful guide.

Life, like a dance, is a harmonious interplay of movement, rhythm, and transitions. The crow, known for its agility and elegance in flight, symbolizes the art of navigating these movements with grace. "The Crow's Dance" encourages us to emulate this graceful dance by moving seamlessly between the different realms of existence.

This message prompts us to recognize that our lives are composed of various dimensions, including the physical, emotional, mental, and spiritual. Each realm has its own rhythm and energy, much like different dance steps in a choreography. Just as the crow effortlessly transitions between the realms of the earth and the sky, we too can learn to navigate life's diverse experiences with poise and adaptability.

"The Crow's Dance" also encourages us to embrace the idea that there is unity in diversity. Life's dance includes moments of joy and sorrow, success and failure, love and loss. Much like the crow's flight patterns, our journey may take us through different emotional, intellectual, and spiritual landscapes. By acknowledging the interconnectedness of these experiences, we can find meaning and purpose in the dance of life.

Moreover, this message inspires us to remain present in each moment of our dance. Just as the crow is fully engaged in its flight, we are encouraged to immerse ourselves in the present, savoring the beauty of each step in our journey. By doing so, we can experience life's richness more fully and appreciate the unique gifts of each realm.

By embracing the diverse experiences that make up our existence and by moving seamlessly between them, we can find harmony, balance, and a deeper sense of purpose in the dance of life.

13
INTUITION

LET YOUR INNER GPS SHAPE YOUR PATH, LISTEN MORE TO YOUR HEART AND INNER KNOWING

MESSAGE:

TRUST YOUR INTUITION, FOR IT IS A GIFT FROM THE CROW'S WORLD, GUIDING YOU WHEN WORDS FAIL.

INVOKE THE CROW TO ENHANCE YOUR INTUITION, TREATING IT LIKE ANY OTHER SENSORY TOOL; THE MORE YOU EMPLOY IT, THE GREATER YOUR TRUST WILL GROW.

The "Intuition" message within the Crow Oracle is a profound reminder of the significance of our inner wisdom and the powerful guidance that comes from trusting our intuitive faculties.

Crows are often associated with a heightened sense of perception and intuition. They possess an innate ability to navigate complex situations and make decisions based on subtle cues and insights. "Intuition" encourages us to tap into this gift from the crow's world and to trust our inner knowing when faced with uncertainty or challenges.

This message underscores the idea that intuition is a valuable source of guidance, especially when traditional means of communication, such as words, may fall short. When we trust our intuition, we are connecting with a deeper and more profound level of understanding that transcends logic and reason. It's as though we are accessing a wisdom that comes from the unseen realms, much like the crow's connection to the mystical.

Moreover, "Intuition" emphasizes the importance of cultivating and honing our intuitive abilities. Just as crows sharpen their perception and intuition through experience, we too can develop our inner guidance system. This involves paying attention to our gut feelings, hunches, and instincts, and learning to differentiate them from fear-based reactions or wishful thinking.

Trusting our intuition also invites us to be present in the moment and to listen to the whispers of our inner world. When we quiet the noise of our minds and external distractions, we create space for intuitive insights to emerge. This message encourages us to embrace mindfulness and self-awareness as tools for enhancing our intuitive capacities.

By trusting this inner guidance system, we can navigate life's complexities with greater confidence and clarity. When we rely on our intuition it will guide us when words fail and help us make choices aligned with our true path.

14
ANCESTRAL CONNECTIONS

EMBRACING EQUILIBRIUM AND COMPASSION

MESSAGE:

THE CROW CARRIES MESSAGES FROM YOUR ANCESTORS; HONOR THEIR WISDOM AND GUIDANCE.

EMBRACE YOUR AGE-OLD POWER AND BESEECH THE CROW TO UNVEIL ANCIENT WISDOM FROM ERAS GONE BY, WITNESSING YOUR INNER STRENGTH FLOURISH.

The "Ancestral Connections" message within the Crow Oracle holds a profound reminder of the importance of honoring and acknowledging the wisdom and guidance of our ancestors, drawing inspiration from the crow as a messenger between the worlds.

Crows have been regarded as spiritual intermediaries in various cultures, often believed to carry messages between the living and the spirit world. "Ancestral Connections" suggests that, like the crow, we can receive messages from our ancestors, who have traversed the realms beyond our mortal existence.

This message encourages us to cultivate a deeper connection with our ancestral lineage, recognizing that the wisdom and experiences of our forebears continue to influence our lives. Just as the crow honors its role as a messenger, we are prompted to acknowledge and respect the guidance that our ancestors offer from the realms beyond.

Ancestral wisdom can manifest in various forms, including family traditions, cultural practices, and even intuitive insights. "Ancestral Connections" encourages us to pay attention to these messages, as they often contain valuable guidance, insights, and lessons passed down through generations.

Moreover, this message reminds us of the intergenerational nature of our existence. We are not isolated beings but rather threads in a larger tapestry of ancestral connections. By honoring and learning from our ancestors, we acknowledge our place within this intricate web of human experience, and we can draw upon their accumulated wisdom to navigate our own lives.

"Ancestral Connections" invites us to embrace the idea that we are never truly alone on our life's journey. We carry with us the collective wisdom and experiences of those who came before us, and their guidance can illuminate our path forward.

15
THE MYSTIC PATH

STAND RESOLUTE, ACKNOWLEDGING THE SHIELD OF SACRED ENERGIES THAT ENVELOPS AND SAFEGUARDS YOU.

MESSAGE:

WALK THE MYSTIC PATH WITH COURAGE, KNOWING THAT THE CROW'S PRESENCE SHIELDS YOU FROM HARM.

AS YOU VENTURE INTO DIFFERENT REALMS ON YOUR SPIRITUAL JOURNEY, REST ASSURED THAT YOU ARE UNDER A PROTECTIVE SHIELD, ALLOWING YOU TO EXPLORE AND ADVANCE FREELY.

"The Mystic Path" message within the Crow Oracle imparts a profound call to embark on a journey of spiritual exploration and growth, likened to the mystic path that crows are believed to tread. This message encourages us to cultivate courage and trust in the protective presence of the crow as we navigate the mystical and unknown realms of existence.

Crows have long held a mystical and symbolic significance in various cultures, often associated with transcendence, wisdom, and a connection to the unseen. "The Mystic Path" invites us to follow in their symbolic footsteps, embracing a path of spiritual enlightenment and self-discovery.

Walking the mystic path requires courage because it often leads us into the unknown, challenging us to confront our fears and doubts. Just as the crow fearlessly explores its surroundings, this message reminds us to venture beyond our comfort zones and explore the depths of our spirituality and inner consciousness.

The crow's presence as a shield from harm suggests that when we embark on the mystic path with sincerity and a genuine quest for knowledge, we are protected from spiritual or emotional harm. It reassures us that the wisdom and guidance we seek are available to us, shielding us from the negative forces or influences that may attempt to deter us.

Furthermore, "The Mystic Path" highlights the importance of trust and intuition on this journey. Just as the crow relies on its instincts to navigate the unseen, we too can trust our inner guidance and intuition to lead us on the right path. This message encourages us to listen to the whispers of our soul and embrace the synchronicities and signs that guide our way.

By walking this path with sincerity and intuition, we can uncover profound insights, connect with our spiritual essence, and find solace in the knowledge that we are shielded from harm.

16
SYNCHRONICITY

SUMMONING THE FOUR ELEMENTS INTO EXISTENCE STABILIZES AND HARMONIZES ENERGIES, PAVING THE WAY FOR SYNCHRONICITIES TO MANIFEST.

MESSAGE:

PAY ATTENTION TO SYNCHRONICITIES, THEY SHOW YOU'RE ON THE RIGHT PATH. REMEBER TO ALWAYS GIVE GRATITUDE FOR THIS WILL BRING UPON MORE SYNCHRONICITIES.

NOTHING HAPPENS BY CHANCE; EVERYTHING IS PREDESTINED, AND SYNCHRONICITIES SERVE AS A PRELUDE TO SIGNIFICANT EVENTS.

The "Synchronicity" message within the Crow Oracle is a profound reminder of the interconnectedness of all things and the meaningful coincidences that often guide us along our life's journey. This message encourages us to be attentive to these synchronicities, as they are seen as signs from the crow, affirming that we are on the right path.

Synchronicity is the occurrence of seemingly unrelated events or experiences that align in a meaningful way, often defying conventional explanations of causality. Just as crows are known for their ability to spot patterns and connections in the world, "Synchronicity" invites us to recognize the significance of these events in our lives.

This message emphasizes the idea that synchronicities are not mere chance occurrences but are, in fact, a form of guidance from a higher source. Much like the crow's messages, they are a means by which the universe communicates with us, affirming that we are in alignment with our true purpose and destiny.

Synchronicities can manifest in various forms, such as meaningful encounters, unexpected opportunities, or repeating patterns or symbols. They often occur when we are open, receptive, and present in the moment. "Synchronicity" encourages us to pay attention to these occurrences, as they may provide valuable insights, affirmations, or confirmations of our path in life.

Furthermore, this message reminds us that synchronicities often serve as markers or guides, directing us toward greater self-awareness and personal growth. When we heed these signs, we are encouraged to embrace our unique journey with confidence and trust, knowing that we are in sync with the flow of life.

By paying attention to synchronicities, we can navigate our journey with a greater sense of purpose, clarity, and confidence, knowing that the universe conspires to guide us toward our highest potential.

17
EMBRACING DARKNESS

WITHOUT THE DARK THERE IS NO LIGHT

MESSAGE:

JUST AS THE CROW SOARS THROUGH THE NIGHT, EMBRACE YOUR SHADOW SELF, FOR IT HOLDS VALUABLE LESSONS.

YOUR FINEST ACHIEVEMENTS EMERGE FROM CONQUERING YOUR DARKEST MOMENTS. AS YOU BASK IN YOUR RADIANCE, RECALL YOUR SHADOWS AND MEND THEM WITH GRATITUDE AND LOVE.

The "Embracing Darkness" message within the Crow Oracle carries a profound and transformative lesson, encouraging us to confront and embrace the hidden aspects of ourselves, often referred to as our shadow self. This message draws inspiration from the crow's ability to soar through the night, traversing the darkness with grace.

In psychology, the concept of the shadow self represents the aspects of our personality that we suppress, deny, or reject because they are deemed unacceptable or uncomfortable. These aspects may include our fears, insecurities, unhealed wounds, and repressed emotions. Much like the crow's ability to navigate the night, "Embracing Darkness" calls upon us to explore the depths of our own inner darkness.

This message challenges us to confront our shadow self with courage and compassion, recognizing that it holds valuable lessons and insights about our true nature. Just as the crow is not defined solely by its daylight appearance but also by its ability to navigate the night, we are multidimensional beings with both light and darkness within us.

By embracing our shadow self, we can gain a deeper understanding of our fears, triggers, and unresolved issues. This self-awareness is a crucial step toward healing and personal growth. It allows us to integrate these shadow aspects, transforming them into sources of strength and wisdom.

Moreover, "Embracing Darkness" reminds us that there is beauty and wisdom to be found in the shadows. Much like the crow's presence in the night adds depth and mystery to its existence, our shadow self can enrich our lives by providing contrast and depth to our experiences. It challenges us to question, explore, and evolve.

When we accept the complexity of our nature and confront our shadow self with openness and courage, we can unlock the valuable lessons and insights it holds, leading to greater self-awareness, healing, and personal growth.

18
THE KEEPER OF SECRETS

ASK THE CROW TO REVEAL THE SECRETS OF THE COSMOS AND BECOME ONE WITH ALL

MESSAGE:

THE SECRETS OF THE COSMOS ARE SACRED AND ACCESSED ONLY BY THOSE DESRVING OF ITS POWER. BE BRAVE AND ASK THE CROW TO REVEAL SECRETS TO HELP YOU ALONG YOUR SPIRITUAL JOURNEY.

GIVE AND TAKE IS REQUIRED WHEN WE ASK FOR SACRED KNOWLEDGE.

"The Keeper of Secrets" message within the Crow Oracle carries a profound lesson about trust, discretion, and the symbolic role of crows as guardians of hidden wisdom and cosmic knowledge.

Crows have been regarded as symbols of mystery and guardianship of esoteric knowledge in various cultures. They are often associated with the idea that they possess deep insights into the mysteries of the universe. "The Keeper of Secrets" message invites us to recognize and trust in the crow's discretion as they safeguard the secrets of the cosmos.

This message encourages us to acknowledge that not all knowledge is meant to be openly shared or readily accessible. Just as crows are selective in their communications, we are called upon to exercise discretion in our own lives, especially when entrusted with sensitive information or profound wisdom.

Trust plays a central role in this message. We are invited to trust in the wisdom of the universe and in the guidance it provides through symbols and signs, such as the presence of crows. It reminds us that there is a vast reservoir of hidden knowledge and insights waiting to be discovered when the time is right.

Moreover, "The Keeper of Secrets" suggests that wisdom is not something to be possessed or hoarded but rather something to be respected and revered. It encourages us to approach knowledge and wisdom with humility and a sense of awe, much like the reverence one might feel for the secrets of the cosmos.

"The Keeper of Secrets" emphasizes the importance of discretion, trust, and reverence for the mysteries of existence. It invites us to recognize the symbolic role of crows as guardians of hidden wisdom and cosmic secrets. By acknowledging the wisdom that crows represent and by trusting in the discretion of the universe, we can tap into a deeper understanding of life's mysteries and approach our own journey with humility and reverence.

19
FLIGHT OF FREEDOM

RELEASE THE SHACKLES THAT TIE YOU DOWN

MESSAGE:

RELEASE THE BURDENS THAT WEIGH YOU DOWN AND SOAR WITH THE CROW IN THE VAST EXPANSE OF FREEDOM.

INHALE DEEPLY, THEN EXHALE, LIBERATING ALL THE AIR FROM YOUR LUNGS, EMBRACING THE PROFOUND FREEDOM WITHIN.

The "Flight of Freedom" message within the Crow Oracle imparts a liberating and transformative lesson, encouraging us to shed the burdens that hold us back and embrace a life of boundless freedom and possibility, much like the crow's graceful flight through the open skies.

Crows are renowned for their agility and freedom in flight, soaring through the air with grace and precision. "Flight of Freedom" draws inspiration from the crow's ability to navigate the world unburdened by limitations, inviting us to release the emotional, mental, and spiritual weights that hinder our own progress.

This message prompts us to reflect on the burdens we carry—be they self-doubt, fear, past regrets, or limiting beliefs. It encourages us to acknowledge these burdens and take steps to release them. Just as the crow takes flight unburdened, we can free ourselves from the weight of our past and the constraints of our own making.

Furthermore, "Flight of Freedom" invites us to step into a state of profound liberation and self-discovery. By shedding our burdens, we create space for new experiences, opportunities, and perspectives. Much like the crow's flight expands into the vast expanse of the open sky, we too can expand our horizons and explore the uncharted territories of our potential.

This message also emphasizes the idea that freedom is a state of mind. It encourages us to cultivate a sense of inner freedom, even in the midst of external challenges. Just as the crow embodies freedom in its graceful flight, we can nurture a sense of empowerment and autonomy over our own lives.

"Flight of Freedom" serves as a powerful reminder to release the burdens that weigh us down and embrace a life of liberation and boundless potential. It inspires us to follow the crow's example and take flight with grace, unburdened by limitations, and with a profound sense of inner freedom. This message encourages us to live a life in which we soar through the vast expanse of possibilities and embrace the transformative power of liberation and self-discovery.

20
THE CIRCLE OF LIFE

ACCEPTING THE CYCLES OF LIFE FOR THEY BRING GROWTH

MESSAGE:

WELCOME THE CYCLES, AS THEY USHER GROWTH. KEEP IN MIND THAT EVERYTHING RETURNS IN DUE TIME; IT'S YOUR ACTIONS WITHIN THESE CYCLES THAT TRULY MATTER.

REFLECT ON YOUR JOURNEY AND HONOR THE CYCLES YOU HAVE BEEN THROUGH TO GET WHERE YOU ARE.

"The Circle of Life" message within the Crow Oracle imparts a timeless and profound lesson about the cyclical nature of existence, drawing inspiration from the crow's flight patterns that trace circular paths in the sky. This message invites us to embrace the natural cycles of life as sources of growth, transformation, and wisdom.

Crows, in their flight patterns, often create circular motions that symbolize the cyclical nature of life, much like the changing seasons, lunar phases, and the rhythm of birth, growth, death, and rebirth that characterize our own existence. "The Circle of Life" encourages us to recognize and honor these cycles as inherent aspects of our journey.

This message emphasizes that life is not a linear journey but a continuous and evolving cycle. Each phase of the cycle brings its own unique lessons, challenges, and opportunities. By embracing these cycles, we can cultivate a deeper understanding of our own growth and evolution.

Moreover, "The Circle of Life" suggests that within each cycle, there is a rhythm and purpose. Just as the crow's flight patterns serve a purpose in its navigation, our own life cycles have significance in shaping our character, resilience, and wisdom. It encourages us to trust in the unfolding of our journey, knowing that each cycle contributes to our personal growth and transformation.

This message also invites us to let go of resistance to change and to find beauty in the ebb and flow of life's cycles. Change can be unsettling, but it is also a source of renewal and opportunity. Like the crow gracefully moves through its circular flight, we can navigate life's changes with grace and resilience.

Embrace the inherent cycles of existence as opportunities for growth and transformation. See the beauty and purpose in the ever-turning wheel of life. By recognizing the cyclical nature of life, we can navigate our journey with greater wisdom, patience, and a deeper sense of connection to the natural rhythms of the universe.

21
THE CROW'S LAUGHTER

LAUGH WITHOUT REASON, LIKE THE CROW THAT LAUGHS ON THE TREE TOPS FOR NO REASON

MESSAGE:

FIND JOY IN THE CROW'S PLAYFUL LAUGHTER, AND LET IT REMIND YOU NOT TO TAKE LIFE TOO SERIOUSLY.

CULTIVATE LAUGHTER INTO YOUR DAY TO DAY LIFE.

"The Crow's Laughter" message within the Crow Oracle imparts a lighthearted and essential lesson about finding joy, embracing playfulness, and maintaining a sense of humor in the midst of life's challenges. This message draws inspiration from the symbolic laughter of the crow, encouraging us not to take life too seriously.

Crows are often seen as playful and intelligent birds, known for their vocalizations that can sometimes sound like laughter. "The Crow's Laughter" message invites us to follow their example by infusing our lives with moments of joy and laughter.

In the hustle and bustle of life, it's easy to become bogged down by responsibilities, stress, and worries. This message reminds us of the importance of maintaining a sense of humor and lightness, even in the face of adversity. Laughter has the power to lift our spirits, reduce stress, and create a sense of connection with others.

Furthermore, "The Crow's Laughter" encourages us to adopt a playful and curious attitude towards life. Just as crows are known for their inquisitive nature, we can approach our experiences with a childlike wonder and openness. This playful mindset can lead to greater creativity, resilience, and adaptability.

This message also highlights the idea that laughter is a universal language that transcends barriers and brings people together. Much like the crow's vocalizations create a sense of community among crows, our laughter can foster connections with others, strengthening relationships and enhancing our social bonds.

"The Crow's Laughter" serves as a gentle reminder to find joy and laughter in our lives, embracing a playful and curious mindset. It encourages us not to take life too seriously, as laughter has the power to uplift our spirits and connect us with others. By following the crow's example and infusing our lives with laughter, we can navigate life's challenges with greater resilience, positivity, and a deeper sense of connection to the world around us.

22
MYSTICAL CONNECTIONS

PURSUE CONNECTIONS THAT ELEVATE YOUR CONSCIOUSNESS TO HIGHER REALMS.

MESSAGE:

EXPLORE MYSTICAL BONDS WITH THOSE ATTUNED TO THE CROW'S MESSAGES.

CULTIVATE YOUR CURRENT CONNECTIONS AND THOSE YET TO FORM, AS EACH CARRIES VALUABLE LESSONS AND OPPORTUNITIES FOR GROWTH.

The "Mystical Connections" message within the Crow Oracle carries a profound reminder of the value of seeking and nurturing meaningful connections with others who share a similar spiritual awareness and attunement to the symbolic messages of the crow.

Crows have long been associated with mysticism and the esoteric, often believed to serve as messengers between the spiritual and earthly realms. "Mystical Connections" encourages us to recognize that there are individuals who, like the crow, possess a deep understanding of these mystical aspects of life.

This message prompts us to seek out and connect with those who resonate with the wisdom and symbolism of the crow. It suggests that by forging connections with kindred spirits who share a similar spiritual or mystical perspective, we can deepen our own understanding and experience of the world.

Moreover, "Mystical Connections" underscores the idea that there is a sense of unity and purpose in connecting with like-minded individuals. Just as crows often gather in flocks, we too can find strength, support, and inspiration in forming communities of individuals who share our spiritual journey.

This message also invites us to be open to the synchronicities and signs that may guide us toward these mystical connections. Much like the crow's presence can be seen as a sign, the universe may send us subtle cues and hints that lead us to those who resonate with our spiritual path.

"Mystical Connections" encourages us to seek out and nurture relationships with individuals who share a similar attunement to the crow's messages and the mystical aspects of life. By connecting with like-minded souls, we can deepen our spiritual journey, find support and inspiration, and embrace the sense of unity and purpose that comes from walking the path of mysticism and symbolism. This message reminds us that there is a profound sense of connection and wisdom to be found in the company of those who share our spiritual journey.

23

DIVINE TIMING

DIVINE TIMING REPRESENTS THE UNIVERSE PROVIDING WHAT YOU CAN HANDLE WHEN YOU'RE FULLY PREPARED.

MESSAGE:

TRUST IN DIVINE TIMING. EVERYTHING IS ALWAYS HAPPENING FOR YOU AND NOT TOU YOU.

ALLOCATE MOMENTS TO EMBRACE WHAT IS, FOR HASTENING INTO SITUATIONS OR TRYING TO FORCE THINGS DISRUPTS THE INNATE RHYTHM OF THE UNIVERSE. PERMIT DIVINE TIMING TO UNFOLD AS IT SHOULD.

The "Divine Timing" message within the Crow Oracle imparts a profound lesson about patience, trust, and the understanding that there is a perfect rhythm and timing to the unfolding of events in our lives, much like the crow's messages, which arrive when the universe deems it necessary.

Crows, as symbols of intuition and cosmic awareness, are believed to carry messages between the realms, often at precisely the right moment. "Divine Timing" encourages us to trust in the universe's orchestration of events and messages, recognizing that everything unfolds according to a higher plan.

This message reminds us that, in our fast-paced world, we may often be in a rush to see results, find answers, or receive guidance. However, like the crow, we are encouraged to be patient and trust that messages and opportunities will manifest in our lives at the most appropriate times.

"Divine Timing" underscores the idea that life's unfolding is not always under our control, and that certain events or insights may require a gestation period. Just as the crow's messages come when the universe deems it necessary, so too do our own revelations and life changes occur when they are meant to.

Moreover, this message encourages us to be attuned to the signs and synchronicities that the universe presents. While we may not have control over when messages arrive, we can cultivate awareness and receptivity, allowing us to recognize and interpret the guidance and opportunities that come our way.

"Divine Timing" invites us to trust in the natural order of life and the universe's perfect timing. It encourages patience and the understanding that, much like the crow's messages, insights and opportunities will come when they are meant to. By embracing this message, we can navigate our journey with greater ease, knowing that the universe's plan unfolds in its own time and that there is a divine order to the events in our lives.

24
INNER ALCHEMY

INVOKE THE CROW'S ASSISTANCE IN HARMONIZING THE FOUR ELEMENTS WITHIN YOURSELF, TO ESTABLISH A CONNECTION TO THE SPIRIT REALM

MESSAGE:

TRANSFORM YOUR INNER SELF THROUGH ALCHEMY, JUST AS THE CROW TRANSFORMS THE MUNDANE INTO THE EXTRAORDINARY.

JUST AS YOUR ANCESTORS RECOGNIZED THE SIGNIFICANCE OF ENGAGING IN ALCHEMY THROUGH WORK AND PRACTICE, YOU TOO SHOULD SEEK THE GUIDANCE OF THE CROW ON YOUR ALCHEMICAL JOURNEY.

The "Inner Alchemy" message within the Crow Oracle imparts a profound lesson about personal transformation and the alchemical process that occurs within us, drawing inspiration from the crow's ability to transform the mundane into the extraordinary.

Alchemy is an ancient philosophical and mystical tradition that seeks to transmute base metals into precious ones and achieve spiritual enlightenment. "Inner Alchemy" encourages us to apply the principles of this tradition to our own lives, focusing on the transformation of our inner selves.

Much like the crow's knack for turning ordinary objects into valuable treasures, this message prompts us to recognize the potential for transformation within ourselves. It suggests that we have the power to transmute our own "base" qualities—such as negative emotions, limiting beliefs, and unproductive behaviors—into qualities that are more "precious" and aligned with our higher selves.

"Inner Alchemy" also highlights the idea that transformation is an ongoing and cyclical process, much like the crow's continuous journey of change and adaptation. It encourages us to embrace the idea that personal growth and self-improvement are lifelong endeavors, and that each stage of our journey holds the potential for transformation.

Furthermore, this message invites us to be mindful of the resources we possess within ourselves for this inner alchemical process. Just as the crow uses its innate intelligence and intuition to transform its surroundings, we can harness our own inner resources, such as self-awareness, introspection, and a commitment to personal development, to facilitate our transformation.

By embracing this message, we can embark on a journey of profound self-transformation and inner enrichment, just as the crow continuously transforms its world.

25
THE HIDDEN PATH

EMRACE THE HIDDEN PATH FOR IT WAS PUT BEFORE YOU FOR A REASON

MESSAGE:

WITHIN THESE HIDDEN REALMS, PROFOUND AND SACRED TRUTHS LIE IN WAIT, EAGER TO REVEAL THEMSELVES TO THOSE WHO DARE TO TREAD THIS MYSTICAL TRAIL.

EXPLORE, DREAM AND DISCOVER AS YOU HEAD DOWN THE HIDDEN PATH.

"The Hidden Path" message within the Crow Oracle invites us to embark on a journey of spiritual exploration and discovery, drawing inspiration from the crow as our guide along this hidden path where profound truths are concealed.

Crows have long been associated with mystery and esoteric knowledge, often serving as messengers between the spiritual and earthly realms. "The Hidden Path" encourages us to recognize the crow's symbolic role as a guide to deeper spiritual understanding.
This message prompts us to acknowledge that there is more to our existence than what meets the eye. Just as crows traverse hidden paths in their search for sustenance and wisdom, we too can explore the hidden aspects of our own spirituality, seeking deeper truths and insights.

"The Hidden Path" also suggests that the journey of spiritual exploration is not always straightforward or readily apparent. It often involves venturing into uncharted territory, questioning established beliefs, and embracing the unknown. Much like the crow's ability to navigate hidden paths, we are encouraged to trust our intuition and inner guidance as we explore the mysteries of the spiritual realm.

Furthermore, this message emphasizes the importance of patience and mindfulness on this hidden path. Spiritual truths and insights may not always be immediately apparent, and they may require time, introspection, and meditation to reveal themselves. Just as the crow patiently searches for hidden treasures, we too can approach our spiritual journey with a sense of patience and dedication.

"The Hidden Path" encourages us to follow the crow along the concealed avenues of spirituality, where profound truths and insights await discovery. It invites us to trust our intuition and inner guidance as we navigate this hidden path, embracing the mysteries of the spiritual realm. By embarking on this journey with patience, curiosity, and an open heart, we can uncover the profound truths that have the potential to transform our lives and deepen our connection to the spiritual aspects of existence.

26
THE CROW'S COUNCIL

THE CROW'S DOOR STANDS WIDE OPEN, INVITING YOU TO APPROACH AND SEEK THE WISDOM IT HOLDS

MESSAGE:

EMBRACE THE PRACTICE OF SEEKING COUNSEL FROM A COUNCIL OF CROWS WHEN CONFRONTED WITH PIVOTAL DECISIONS IN YOUR LIFE.

OUR GROWTH ACCELERATES WHEN WE JOIN FORCES WITH KINDRED SPIRITS WHO SHARE OUR OUTLOOK AND POSSESS PURE HEARTS. TO ADVANCE ON YOUR SPIRITUAL JOURNEY, ACTIVELY SEEK OUT THOSE WHO RESONATE WITH YOUR BELIEFS AND ASPIRATIONS, FOR TOGETHER, YOU CAN FORGE A PATH OF PROFOUND PROGRESS.

"The Crow's Council" message within the Crow Oracle imparts a powerful lesson about seeking guidance, wisdom, and collective insight when confronted with significant decisions in life. This message draws inspiration from the idea that crows often gather in groups, sharing knowledge and collaborating.

Crows are highly intelligent birds known for their capacity to communicate and cooperate with one another. "The Crow's Council" encourages us to recognize the value of collective wisdom and collaboration when we face important choices and dilemmas.

This message prompts us to consider seeking advice and counsel from a diverse group of individuals who possess different perspectives and expertise. Just as the crow's council benefits from the input of various members, we too can benefit from the wisdom and insights of those with different backgrounds, experiences, and viewpoints.

"The Crow's Council" also underscores the idea that important decisions are often best made when we have access to a variety of perspectives. It encourages us to be open to feedback, to engage in meaningful discussions, and to consider the potential consequences and implications of our choices from multiple angles.

Furthermore, this message invites us to recognize that we don't have to navigate life's challenges and decisions in isolation. Just as crows collaborate to achieve their goals, we can seek the support and guidance of a trusted council of friends, mentors, or advisors to help us make informed and thoughtful choices.

By drawing upon the diverse perspectives and expertise of our own "crow's council," we can navigate life's complexities with greater clarity, confidence, and a deeper sense of collective wisdom.

27
THE THRESHOLD

CROSSING THE THRESHOLD WITH UNWAVERING CONFIDENCE

MESSAGE:

EMBARK ON A JOURNEY INTO THE ENIGMATIC AND UNCHARTED TERRITORIES OF THE UNKNOWN, WHERE THE POSSIBILITIES FOR DISCOVERY AND TRANSFORMATION ARE BOUNDLESS.

DISCOVER WITHIN YOURSELF THE RESERVOIR OF STRENGTH NECESSARY TO MAKE DECISIONS WHEN THEY ARE MOST NEEDED. IN MOMENTS OF UNCERTAINTY AND CHOICE, TAP INTO YOUR INNER RESOLVE, DRAWING UPON THE WELLSPRING OF COURAGE AND DETERMINATION THAT EMPOWERS YOU TO NAVIGATE THE PATH AHEAD WITH CLARITY AND CONVICTION.

"The Threshold" message within the Crow Oracle is a compelling invitation to embrace the ambiguity and mystery of life, drawing inspiration from the crow's role as a messenger between different realms and dimensions.

The threshold symbolizes a transitional space, a point of departure from the known into the unknown. It is a liminal space where possibilities and opportunities abound. "The Threshold" encourages us to stand at this precipice, where the crow beckons us to explore the uncharted territories of existence.

This message prompts us to recognize that life often presents us with moments of decision and change, akin to standing at a crossroads or a threshold. These moments can be both exhilarating and daunting, much like the sensation of the crow's presence as a guide between worlds.

"The Threshold" invites us to embrace the idea that the unknown holds a wealth of potential and growth. It encourages us to step beyond our comfort zones, to question our assumptions, and to venture into the realms of exploration and discovery.

Furthermore, this message emphasizes the importance of trust and intuition when standing at the threshold. Just as the crow relies on its instincts and cosmic awareness to navigate between realms, we too can trust our inner guidance and intuition to lead us on the right path when facing life's uncertainties.

"The Threshold" inspires us to stand at the precipice of the unknown with courage and curiosity, much like the crow beckoning us to explore new realms. It encourages us to embrace life's moments of transition and change as opportunities for growth and discovery. By stepping beyond the threshold and into the realms of the unfamiliar, we can unlock the hidden potentials and possibilities that await us on our journey through life.

28
THE CROWS FEATHER

ABSORB THE ANCIENT SECRETS IMPRINTED IN THE CROWS FEATHER

MESSAGE:

WHEN YOU FIND A CROW'S FEATHER, KNOW THAT IT IS A GIFT OF PROTECTION AND GUIDANCE, CARRYING ANCIENT SECRETS.

KEEP A CROW'S FEATHER AND INCORPORATE IT IN YOUR ALTAR SO YOU CAN CONNECT WITH THE ANCIENT WISDOM IMPRINTED WITHIN IT.

"The Crow's Feather" message within the Crow Oracle carries a beautiful and symbolic significance, emphasizing the idea that when we encounter a crow's feather, it is not just a simple object but a profound gift of protection and guidance from the natural world.

Feathers have held deep symbolic meaning in various cultures throughout history, often associated with spirituality, transcendence, and messages from the divine. The crow, with its spiritual and mystical connotations, further elevates the significance of finding one of its feathers.

This message prompts us to recognize that the natural world often communicates with us in subtle but powerful ways. When we discover a crow's feather, it serves as a reminder that we are interconnected with the world around us and that nature can offer us guidance and protection.

"The Crow's Feather" invites us to embrace the idea that there is a sense of providence or serendipity in these encounters. It suggests that finding such a feather is not a random occurrence but a deliberate message from the universe, offering us a sense of comfort and assurance.

Furthermore, this message encourages us to acknowledge the protective and guiding qualities of the crow as symbolized by its feather. Much like crows are known to watch over their territories and offer guidance through their vocalizations and behaviors, the presence of a crow's feather can serve as a protective and guiding force in our lives.

When we encounter a crow's feather, we can embrace it as a meaningful gift, a symbol of connection with the mystical and the assurance that we are being watched over and guided in our life's path.

29
THE WISDOM OF SILENCE

TAKE ON THE ENERGY OF SILENCE, BECOME THE ENERGY COMPLETELY

MESSAGE:

LEARN THE PROFOUND AND AGELESS WISDOM OF SILENCE IF YOU SEEK TO ACCESS DEEPER INSIGHTS AND CONNECT WITH HIGHER ENERGIES.

BE STILL AND OBSERVE AS DOES THE CROW FOR IN THIS STATE OF AWARENESS YOU ALLOW FOR HIGHER ENERGIES TO FLOW WITHIN YOU.

"The Wisdom of Silence" message within the Crow Oracle imparts a profound lesson about the value of stillness, introspection, and the profound insights that can arise when we embrace the silence within, drawing inspiration from the crow's ability to observe and learn in silence.

Crows are known for their capacity to silently watch, listen, and learn from their surroundings. "The Wisdom of Silence" encourages us to follow their example and discover the profound wisdom that emerges when we quiet our minds and create space for inner reflection.

This message prompts us to recognize the frenetic pace of modern life, often filled with noise, distractions, and constant activity. In contrast, it invites us to carve out moments of silence and solitude, where we can turn our attention inward and attune ourselves to the subtle truths that lie beneath the surface.

"The Wisdom of Silence" suggests that in moments of stillness, we can access deeper insights, intuition, and inner wisdom. It encourages us to cultivate mindfulness and presence, allowing us to observe our thoughts, emotions, and surroundings with greater clarity and depth.

Furthermore, this message highlights the idea that silence is not an absence of meaning but a reservoir of wisdom waiting to be tapped into. Much like the crow's silent observation leads to learning and adaptation, our own moments of introspection and silence can lead to personal growth and self-discovery.

"The Wisdom of Silence" inspires us to embrace the value of stillness, introspection, and inner reflection in our lives. It encourages us to follow the crow's example and discover the profound insights that arise when we create space for silence. By cultivating mindfulness and presence, we can navigate life's complexities with greater clarity, intuition, and a deeper connection to our own inner wisdom.

30

THE GUARDIAN

EMBRACE THE NOBLE ROLE OF A STEADFAST GUARDIAN WITHIN THE INTRICATE TAPESTRY OF YOUR OWN REALM

MESSAGE:

DEDICATE YOURSELF TO THE SOLEMN DUTY OF SAFEGUARDING ALL THAT IS CHERISHED AND PRECIOUS IN THE INTRICATE WEB OF YOUR EXISTENCE.

UNDERSTAND WHAT IS IMPORTANT TO YOU. RELEASE THE OLD PATTERNS THAT KEEP YOU FROM TAKING CARE OF WHAT YOU CARE ABOUT.

The "Guardian" message within the Crow Oracle imparts a powerful lesson about responsibility, protection, and the importance of safeguarding what is precious to us, drawing inspiration from the crow's role as a protector of its territory and kin.

Crows are known for their keen sense of vigilance and their commitment to protecting their flock and territory. "The Guardian" encourages us to emulate the crow's sense of guardianship in our own lives, taking responsibility for what we hold dear and cherish.

This message prompts us to reflect on what is most important to us, whether it's our loved ones, our values, our dreams, or our inner peace, and to take proactive steps to protect and preserve these aspects of our lives. Much like the crow watches over its realm, we too can become guardians of what matters most to us.

"The Guardian" also underscores the idea that protection is not solely a physical act but can extend to emotional and spiritual realms as well. It encourages us to defend our boundaries, values, and well-being, recognizing that these aspects of our lives are worth safeguarding.

Furthermore, this message invites us to cultivate a sense of responsibility and commitment to our roles as guardians. Just as the crow takes its duties seriously, we too can approach our roles as protectors with dedication, integrity, and an unwavering sense of purpose.

"The Guardian" inspires us to embrace the role of protector and guardian in our own lives, much like the crow's commitment to safeguarding its realm. It encourages us to take responsibility for what is dear to us and to defend our boundaries, values, and well-being with dedication and commitment. By adopting the crow's sense of vigilance and guardianship, we can navigate life's challenges with a profound sense of responsibility and an unwavering commitment to protecting what is most precious to us.

31

THE CROW'S EYE

CALL ON THE CROW'S EYE TO REVEAL THE MYSTERY OF THE OTHER REALMS

MESSAGE:

OPEN YOUR INNER EYE, ONLY THROUGH THIS EXPANDED VISION WILL YOU SEE THE REALMS BEYOND THE CONFINES OF THE PHYSICAL WORLD.

TURN YOUR EYE WITHIN SO YOU TOO CAN SEE THE REALITY OF WHAT IS.

"The Crow's Eye" message within the Crow Oracle imparts a profound lesson about perception, insight, and the capacity to see beyond the surface of reality, drawing inspiration from the crow's reputation for keen observation and its symbolic role as a messenger between realms.

Crows are celebrated for their remarkable vision and perception, which allows them to navigate both the physical and spiritual worlds. "The Crow's Eye" encourages us to open our own inner eye, our capacity for heightened awareness and intuitive insight, so that we may perceive the deeper truths and realities that often elude ordinary sight.

This message prompts us to recognize that the world is filled with layers of meaning, symbolism, and interconnectedness. By honing our inner vision, we can access a deeper level of understanding and awareness, akin to the crow's ability to see beyond the immediate and into the hidden aspects of existence.

"The Crow's Eye" suggests that this inner sight is not bound by the limitations of the physical world but can extend into the realm of the unseen, the symbolic, and the spiritual. It encourages us to trust our intuition and to seek meaning beyond the surface, knowing that profound insights often lie beneath.

Furthermore, this message invites us to cultivate mindfulness and presence in our daily lives, allowing us to observe our surroundings and experiences with greater depth and clarity. By doing so, we can develop a more profound sense of awareness, much like the crow's vigilant gaze.

"The Crow's Eye" inspires us to open our inner eye, allowing us to perceive the world with heightened awareness and insight. It encourages us to trust our intuition, seek deeper meaning, and embrace the interconnectedness of all things. By honing our inner vision, we can navigate life with a deeper understanding of the subtle truths and hidden realities that shape our existence, much like the crow's vision extends beyond the physical world into the realms of symbolism and the unseen.

32
THE ELEMENTAL CONNECTION

CONNECT WITH THE ELEMENTS AND ACTIVATE YOUR POWER

MESSAGE:

RECOGNIZE YOUR PROFOUND CONNECTION TO THE ELEMENTS TO DISCOVER THE PROFOUND HARMONY THAT THREADS YOUR EXISTENCE TO THE VERY ESSENCE OF THE WORLD.

HARNESSING YOUR INNER POWER BY CONNECTING WITH THE ELEMENTS.

"The Elemental Connection" message within the Crow Oracle invites us to acknowledge and deepen our connection to the natural world and the fundamental forces of nature. This message draws inspiration from the crow's innate attunement to the elements.

Crows are creatures of the earth, air, and sky, often seen as symbols of balance and harmony within the natural world. "The Elemental Connection" encourages us to recognize our own inherent connection to the elements: earth, water, fire, air, and spirit, and to embrace this connection as a source of grounding, wisdom, and inspiration.

This message prompts us to reflect on our relationship with the environment and the ways in which the elements influence our lives. It encourages us to observe and appreciate the subtle ways in which the natural world interacts with our existence, much like the crow is attuned to the forces of nature.

"The Elemental Connection" also underscores the idea that we are not separate from nature but an integral part of it. It invites us to foster a sense of reverence and stewardship for the elements, recognizing that our well-being is deeply intertwined with the health and balance of the natural world.

Furthermore, this message suggests that by acknowledging our elemental connection, we can tap into a deeper source of wisdom and inspiration. The elements have long been associated with archetypal qualities and symbolic meanings. By aligning ourselves with these elemental energies, we can access profound insights and a greater sense of harmony in our lives.

"The Elemental Connection" inspires us to recognize and honor our connection to the fundamental forces of nature, much like the crow's attunement to the elements. It encourages us to embrace our role as stewards of the earth and to find wisdom, balance, and inspiration in our elemental connection. By fostering a deeper relationship with the natural world, we can navigate life with a greater sense of harmony and a profound understanding of the elemental forces that shape our existence.

33
THE INTERCONNECTED WEB

PLAY YOUR PART IN THE GRAND CONNECTED WEB

MESSAGE:

OBSERVE HOW EACH BEING PLAYS A UNIQUE AND VITAL PART, CONTRIBUTING TO THE HARMONY OF THE WHOLE. IN THIS INTERCONNECTED DANCE, FIND THE PROFOUND BEAUTY OF UNITY AND SHARED PURPOSE.

EMBRACE YOUR PART AND CONTRIBUTE TO THE ALL IS ONE CONCEPT AND FEEL YOUR CONNECTION TO THE UNIVERSE.

"The Interconnected Web" message within the Crow Oracle conveys a profound lesson about recognizing the intricate tapestry of existence, wherein every being, like the crow, has a vital role to play in the interconnected web of life.

Crows, as creatures deeply woven into ecosystems, symbolize the interconnectedness of all living things. "The Interconnected Web" encourages us to see beyond surface appearances and acknowledge the interdependence that characterizes our world.

This message prompts us to cultivate a holistic perspective, one that appreciates how every living being, from the smallest microorganisms to the largest creatures, contributes to the balance and harmony of the natural world. Just as the crow plays a role in maintaining ecological equilibrium, we too are part of a broader cosmic tapestry.

"The Interconnected Web" invites us to embrace the idea that our actions and choices ripple through this web, influencing the well-being of other beings and the planet itself. It encourages us to consider the consequences of our actions and to make choices that align with the greater good.

Furthermore, this message underscores the importance of empathy and compassion. When we recognize our interconnectedness with all living things, we become more attuned to the suffering and well-being of others. Much like the crow's presence in its ecosystem, our actions can have a positive impact on the world when rooted in empathy and care.

"The Interconnected Web" inspires us to acknowledge and honor the intricate connections that bind all living beings together in the tapestry of existence. It encourages us to adopt a holistic perspective, make conscious choices that consider the well-being of the broader web of life, and cultivate empathy and compassion for all beings. By embracing our role in this interconnected web, we can navigate life with a profound sense of responsibility and a commitment to nurturing the harmony of existence, much like the crow does within its ecological community.

34

THE COSMIC WHISPERS

*UNCOVER TIMELESS KNOWLEDGE,
ALL IN DIVINE TIMING*

MESSAGE:

IN THE COSMIC STILLNESS, HEED ETHEREAL MURMURS BEARING THE UNIVERSES SECRETS. PATIENT DECODING REVEALS TIMELESS WISDOM, CONNECTING YOU TO PROFOUND TRUTHS.

PAY ATTENTION TO THE UNIVERSES WHISPERS AS EACH SIGN, THOUGHT, IDEA CARRIES SOMETHING SACRED WITH IT.

"The Cosmic Whispers" message within the Crow Oracle imparts a profound lesson about tuning into the subtle and universal wisdom that surrounds us, much like the crow's symbolic connection to the cosmos.

Crows, with their mystical associations and role as messengers, are often seen as intermediaries between the earthly and cosmic realms. "The Cosmic Whispers" encourages us to adopt a receptive and attentive mindset, akin to the crow's ability to hear messages from the cosmos.

This message prompts us to recognize that the universe communicates with us in subtle and often symbolic ways. It encourages us to pay attention to synchronicities, signs, and the whispers of intuition, as they may hold the keys to profound insights and hidden truths.

"The Cosmic Whispers" suggests that the cosmos itself is a wellspring of wisdom, and by listening deeply, we can tap into the universal knowledge that surrounds us. It invites us to embrace a sense of wonder and curiosity about the mysteries of existence, much like the crow's own connection to the enigmatic and unseen forces of the cosmos.

Furthermore, this message underscores the idea that the universe is constantly in communication with us, offering guidance and support on our life's journey. By tuning into the cosmic whispers, we can navigate life with a deeper sense of purpose and alignment with the greater cosmic plan.

"The Cosmic Whispers" inspires us to listen to the subtle and universal messages that surround us, much like the crow's role as a messenger between realms. It encourages us to be attentive to synchronicities and intuitive insights, as they may hold the secrets of the universe. By embracing a sense of wonder and curiosity about the cosmic mysteries, we can navigate life with a profound sense of connection to the cosmos and a deeper understanding of our place within it.

35

THE SACRED OFFERING

TRANSFORMING THROUGH GRATITUDE

MESSAGE:

HONOR THE CROW AS MESSENGERS OF ANCIENT WISDOM WITH HUMBLE TRIBUTES, FORGING A SACRED CONNECTION AND DEEPENING YOUR BOND WITH THEIR PROFOUND GUIDANCE.

MAKE GRATITUDE PART OF YOUR DAILY PRACTICE AND SEE HOW YOUR WORLD STARTS TO TURN.

"The Sacred Offering" message within the Crow Oracle imparts a beautiful lesson about gratitude, reciprocity, and the act of acknowledging the wisdom and guidance we receive, much like the offerings made to the crow as a symbol of appreciation.

Crows, with their symbolic roles and mystical connotations, are often seen as recipients of offerings in various cultures and traditions. "The Sacred Offering" encourages us to embrace the practice of expressing gratitude for the wisdom, guidance, and protection we receive in our lives, whether from the crow or other sources.

This message prompts us to recognize the importance of acknowledging the support and insights that come our way. It invites us to cultivate a sense of gratitude for the lessons and opportunities that have shaped our journey, and to express that gratitude through meaningful acts of offering.

"The Sacred Offering" suggests that making offerings is not merely a physical gesture but a symbolic act of reciprocity. By offering our gratitude and appreciation, we engage in a sacred exchange that strengthens our connection with the source of wisdom and guidance, whether it be the crow or the broader forces of the universe.

Furthermore, this message underscores the idea that the act of giving can be a deeply spiritual and transformative practice. It encourages us to cultivate a mindset of abundance, recognizing that when we give with an open heart, we receive in return a sense of fulfillment and a deepened connection to the wisdom and guidance that enrich our lives.

"The Sacred Offering" inspires us to express gratitude and appreciation for the wisdom and guidance we receive. It encourages us to cultivate a practice of giving and receiving with an open heart, deepening our connection to the sources of wisdom and support in our lives. By embracing this message, we can navigate life with a profound sense of reciprocity and a heightened awareness of the blessings that surround us.

36

THE CROW'S FLIGHT

FLY WITH THE CROW THROUGH REALMS TO GAIN WISDOM AND DOWNLOADS INTO YOUR DNA

MESSAGE:

TAKE FLIGHT WITH THE CROW IN YOUR DREAMS AND MEDITATIONS TO EXPLORE OTHER REALMS.

TAKE NOTICE OF THE CROWS FLIGHT AND ALLOW YOUR INNER BEING TO CONNECT WITH THEM AND THE HIGHER REALMS.

"The Crow's Flight" message within the Crow Oracle imparts a captivating lesson about the power of imagination, meditation, and the boundless exploration of consciousness, drawing inspiration from the crow's symbolic ability to traverse between different realms.

Crows, with their mystical associations and role as messengers, are often seen as guides to the realms beyond the ordinary. "The Crow's Flight" encourages us to tap into our own imagination and inner realms, akin to taking flight with the crow in our dreams and meditations, to explore the uncharted territories of our consciousness.

This message prompts us to recognize that our minds hold the potential for limitless exploration. Just as the crow soars through the skies and between worlds, we too can embark on journeys of discovery within our own inner landscapes. Through meditation, visualization, and dream work, we can access realms of insight, creativity, and spiritual connection.

"The Crow's Flight" suggests that these inner journeys are not confined by the limitations of the physical world but offer us a gateway to deeper understanding and self-discovery. It encourages us to trust our intuition, imagination, and the symbolism that emerges during these flights of consciousness.

Furthermore, this message underscores the idea that exploration of our inner realms can be transformative. Much like the crow's flights lead to new perspectives and insights, our own inner journeys can lead to personal growth, expanded awareness, and a profound sense of connection to the mysteries of existence.

"The Crow's Flight" encourages us to embrace the power of imagination, visualization, and symbolism as tools for self-discovery and spiritual connection. By venturing into these inner realms, we can navigate life with a deeper sense of insight, creativity, and a profound connection to the hidden dimensions of existence.

37
THE KEEPER OF BALANCE

*LEARN BALANCE FROM THE CROW
IT'S YOUR INNATE PATH*

MESSAGE:

BALANCE IS THE THREAD THAT WEAVES HARMONY. NURTURING EQUILIBRIUM IS THE KEYSTONE TO A FULFILLED EXISTENCE.

FIND THE BALANCE WITHIN, AND THE WORLD AROUND YOU FALLS INTO PLACE.

In the grand design of existence, balance is the unspoken orchestrator, harmonizing the rhythms of life. The Keeper of Balance, symbolized by the wise Crow, imparts a timeless message: maintain equilibrium in your life, for it is the fulcrum upon which your well-being rests.

The Crow, with its contrasting black plumage and penetrating gaze, serves as a poignant reminder that life is a delicate dance between light and shadow, joy and sorrow, work and rest. Its presence encourages us to tread the middle path, where extremes give way to moderation, and harmony emerges from the convergence of opposites.

In the bustling chaos of the modern world, finding and preserving balance can be a profound challenge. Yet, the Crow's teachings implore us to navigate the turbulent waters of existence with grace and poise. By doing so, we unlock a reservoir of resilience, inner peace, and clarity.

Maintaining balance extends beyond mere physical equilibrium; it encompasses emotional stability, mental clarity, and spiritual harmony. The Keeper of Balance invites us to introspect, identifying the areas in our lives that yearn for equilibrium. Is it the incessant demands of work encroaching upon our personal time? Or perhaps, the torrent of emotions drowning out our inner serenity?

Just as the Crow gracefully rides the currents of the winds, we too can learn to ride the waves of life's challenges without losing our footing. It is through self-awareness, mindful choices, and a commitment to self-care that we honor the message of the Keeper of Balance.

When we heed this message, we find ourselves better equipped to navigate the ever-shifting landscapes of our existence. We become adept at adjusting our sails to both calm and stormy seas, never losing sight of our true course.

Ultimately, the Keeper of Balance's message resonates not only in our individual lives but also in the broader context of our interconnected world. In seeking equilibrium within ourselves, we contribute to the collective equilibrium of humanity and the planet.

38

THE CYCLE OF REBIRTH

WE VIBRATE IN INFNITE SPACE AND TIME

MESSAGE:

EMBRACE THE CYCLE OF DEATH AND REBIRTH, KNOWING THAT LIKE THE CROW, YOU ARE ETERNAL.

MEDITATE TO BECOME ONE WITH THE CROW.

"The Crow's Flight" message within the Crow Oracle imparts a captivating lesson about the power of imagination, meditation, and the boundless exploration of consciousness, drawing inspiration from the crow's symbolic ability to traverse between different realms.

Crows, with their mystical associations and role as messengers, are often seen as guides to the realms beyond the ordinary. "The Crow's Flight" encourages us to tap into our own imagination and inner realms, akin to taking flight with the crow in our dreams and meditations, to explore the uncharted territories of our consciousness.

This message prompts us to recognize that our minds hold the potential for limitless exploration. Just as the crow soars through the skies and between worlds, we too can embark on journeys of discovery within our own inner landscapes. Through meditation, visualization, and dreamwork, we can access realms of insight, creativity, and spiritual connection.

"The Crow's Flight" suggests that these inner journeys are not confined by the limitations of the physical world but offer us a gateway to deeper understanding and self-discovery. It encourages us to trust our intuition, imagination, and the symbolism that emerges during these flights of consciousness.

Furthermore, this message underscores the idea that exploration of our inner realms can be transformative. Much like the crow's flights lead to new perspectives and insights, our own inner journeys can lead to personal growth, expanded awareness, and a profound sense of connection to the mysteries of existence.

"The Crow's Flight" inspires us to take flight with the crow in our dreams and meditations, exploring the vast and uncharted territories of our inner consciousness. It encourages us to embrace the power of imagination, visualization, and symbolism as tools for self-discovery and spiritual connection. By venturing into these inner realms, we can navigate life with a deeper sense of insight, creativity, and a profound connection to the hidden dimensions of existence.

39
THE COSMIC CONNECTION

AS ABOVE - SO BELOW

MESSAGE:

CONNECT WITH THE COSMOS AS THE CROW DOES, FOR IT IS YOUR BIRTHRIGHT TO BE ONE WITH THE UNIVERSE.

ALIGN WITH THE REALITY OF ONENESS AND ANCHOR IT TO YOUR REALITY.

The Cosmic Connection" message within the Crow Oracle imparts a profound lesson about the disconnectedness of all life, the vast cosmos, and our inherent connection to the universe, drawing inspiration from the crow's symbolic role as a messenger between the earthly and cosmic realms.

Crows, with their mystical associations and cosmic significance, symbolize the idea that all beings are intrinsically linked to the universe. "The Cosmic Connection" encourages us to acknowledge and embrace our birthright to be one with the cosmos, recognizing that we are not separate from the grand tapestry of existence but integral parts of it.

This message prompts us to shift our perspective from a limited, individual view of the world to a more expansive understanding of our place in the cosmos. It invites us to contemplate the mysteries of the universe and to realize that the same cosmic forces that govern the heavens also course through our own beings.

"The Cosmic Connection" suggests that our connection to the cosmos is not merely a conceptual idea but a visceral and profound reality. It encourages us to engage in practices such as stargazing, meditation, and cosmic contemplation to deepen our awareness of this connection.

Furthermore, this message underscores the idea that by recognizing our cosmic connection, we can tap into a wellspring of wisdom, inspiration, and a sense of purpose. It invites us to view ourselves as co-creators in the unfolding story of the universe, contributing to its ongoing evolution.

"The Cosmic Connection" inspires us to embrace our inherent connection to the universe, much like the crow's role as a messenger between realms. It encourages us to transcend narrow boundaries and embrace a broader understanding of existence. By acknowledging our cosmic birthright, we can navigate life with a sense of wonder, purpose, and a profound connection to the vast cosmic forces that shape our reality.

40
THE CROW'S GUIDANCE

FOLLOW YOUR INNER GPS WITH THE CROW'S GUIDANCE

MESSAGE:

THE CROW IS YOUR ETERNAL GUIDE, LEADING YOU THROUGH THE REALMS OF EXISTENCE.

EMBRACE THE ETERNAL ACCESS TO THE CROW'S ABILITY TO GUIDE US.

"The Crow's Guidance" message within the Crow Oracle imparts a profound and comforting lesson about the enduring presence of guidance and support in our lives, drawing inspiration from the crow's symbolic role as a messenger and guide between different realms of existence.

Crows are often seen as symbols of guidance, protection, and wisdom, and "The Crow's Guidance" encourages us to embrace the idea that we are not alone on our life's journey. Instead, we have an eternal guide in the form of the crow, leading us through the various realms of existence.

This message prompts us to recognize that guidance and support are constants in our lives, even in times of uncertainty or change. Much like the crow's unwavering presence in the natural world, we can trust that there is a guiding force at work, offering us direction and insight.

"The Crow's Guidance" suggests that this guidance is not limited to the physical world but extends into the spiritual and unseen realms. It encourages us to be open to messages, signs, and intuitive insights that can provide us with a sense of direction and purpose.

Furthermore, this message underscores the idea that the crow's guidance is eternal, transcending the boundaries of time and space. It invites us to cultivate a sense of trust in the wisdom of the universe, knowing that our path is illuminated by the eternal guidance of the crow.

"The Crow's Guidance" inspires us to embrace the idea that we have an eternal guide, much like the crow, leading us through the realms of existence. It encourages us to trust in the presence of guidance and support in our lives, both seen and unseen. By doing so, we can navigate life's complexities with a profound sense of direction, purpose, and the assurance that we are always on the right path, guided by the wisdom of the crow.

41
THE SACRED DANCE

FOLLOW THE SACRED FLOW AND MOVEMENT OF THE CROW'S DANCE

MESSAGE:

JOIN THE CROW IN THE SACRED DANCE OF LIFE, WHERE EACH STEP IS A MESSAGE FROM THE DIVINE.

LISTEN TO YOUR HEARTS RHYTHM.

"The Sacred Dance" message within the Crow Oracle imparts a beautiful and spiritual lesson about the interconnections of life, the profound nature of existence, and the idea that every step we take is a form of communication with the divine, drawing inspiration from the crow's symbolic role as a messenger and guide between realms.

Crows are often seen as symbols of mysticism and cosmic awareness, and "The Sacred Dance" encourages us to recognize that life itself is a sacred and intricate dance, where every action, choice, and moment holds a deeper meaning and connection to the divine.

This message prompts us to adopt a more mindful and reverent approach to our daily lives. It invites us to view each step we take, whether literal or metaphorical, as an opportunity to communicate with the divine and to participate in the sacred dance of existence.

"The Sacred Dance" suggests that our experiences, relationships, and actions are all interconnected, forming part of a larger cosmic choreography. It encourages us to be present in the moment, to listen to the rhythm of our hearts, and to move in harmony with the flow of life.

Furthermore, this message underscores the idea that by engaging in the sacred dance of life, we can access profound insights, wisdom, and a deeper sense of connection to the divine. It invites us to find joy and purpose in each step we take, knowing that it is a message from the universe itself.

"The Sacred Dance" inspires us to embrace the idea that life is a sacred and interconnected dance, much like the crow's role as a messenger between realms. It encourages us to be mindful and reverent in our actions, recognizing that every step we take is a form of communication with the divine. By participating fully in this sacred dance of existence, we can navigate life with a profound sense of purpose, meaning, and a deeper connection to the mysteries of the cosmos.

42
THE VEIL OF ILLUSION

RIP THAT BAND AID OFF SO YOU CAN FINALLY START LIVING YOUR TRUTH

MESSAGE:

LIFT THE VEIL OF ILLUSION, AND THE CROW WILL REVEAL THE TRUTH THAT LIES BENEATH.

SEE BEYOND THE REALITY WE LIVE IN, ITS TIME TO EXPLORE WHAT YOU CANT SEE IN THE PHYSICAL.

The Veil of Illusion" message within the Crow Oracle imparts a profound and transformative lesson about perception, truth, and the idea that, much like the crow's vision, we can pierce through the illusions that often cloud our understanding of reality.

Crows are often associated with wisdom and insight, and "The Veil of Illusion" encourages us to cultivate a deeper discernment, much like the crow's ability to see through the surface and into the hidden truths of existence.

This message prompts us to recognize that our perception of reality can sometimes be distorted by preconceptions, biases, and the illusions we construct. It invites us to be open to the possibility that there is more to the world than meets the eye and that the truth often lies beneath the surface.

"The Veil of Illusion" suggests that by lifting the veil of our own illusions—whether they be self-limiting beliefs, societal conditioning, or narrow perspectives—we can gain access to a deeper understanding of ourselves and the world around us. It encourages us to question assumptions and be willing to see beyond the facades we encounter.

Furthermore, this message underscores the idea that truth is not fixed but often multifaceted and layered. Just as the crow's keen perception allows it to navigate its environment with clarity, our willingness to lift the veil of illusion can lead to greater insight, wisdom, and authenticity in our lives.

"The Veil of Illusion" inspires us to pierce through the illusions that cloud our perception, much like the crow's ability to reveal hidden truths. It encourages us to embrace a more discerning and open-minded approach to life, allowing us to navigate reality with a deeper understanding of the multifaceted nature of truth. By lifting the veil of illusion, we can uncover the authentic, transformative, and liberating aspects of our existence, just as the crow reveals the secrets of the cosmos beneath the surface of the ordinary.

43

THE ETERNAL MESSENGER

RELY ON THE CROW TO BRING YOU ADVICE AND CLARITY AT JUST THE RIGHT TIME

MESSAGE:

KNOW THAT THE CROW IS AN ETERNAL MESSENGER, BRINGING YOU WISDOM FROM THE COSMOS

LEAN INTO THE MESSAGES THAT ARE DELIVERED BY THE CROW. GIVE THANKS FOR EACH MESSAGE, AS THEY ARE SACRED.

"The Eternal Messenger" message within the Crow Oracle imparts a profound lesson about the timeless and enduring nature of wisdom, drawing inspiration from the crow's symbolic role as a messenger between realms.

Crows have been revered as symbols of wisdom and insight across cultures and centuries. "The Eternal Messenger" encourages us to recognize that the wisdom the crow brings is not bound by time or space. Instead, it is a timeless and eternal source of guidance that originates from the cosmic realm.

This message prompts us to embrace the idea that the crow's role as a messenger is not limited to the here and now. It invites us to perceive the crow as a conduit for wisdom from the cosmos—a bridge between the earthly and spiritual realms.

"The Eternal Messenger" suggests that the wisdom we receive from the crow is not fleeting but endures, offering us timeless insights that resonate across generations. It encourages us to honor and preserve this wisdom, recognizing its profound and enduring value.

Furthermore, this message underscores the idea that the crow's messages are not limited to one particular moment in our lives but are part of a larger, cosmic conversation. It invites us to be open to receiving these messages with gratitude, knowing that they carry the wisdom of the universe.

"The Eternal Messenger" inspires us to embrace the crow as an eternal conduit of wisdom, much like the crow's role as a messenger between realms. It encourages us to recognize the timeless and enduring nature of the insights we receive and to honor the wisdom that transcends time and space. By doing so, we can navigate life with a profound sense of connection to the eternal and cosmic forces that shape our existence.

44
THE CROW'S BLESSING

THE CROW'S BLESSINGS ARE WITH YOU ON YOUR JOURNEY BETWEEN REALMS

MESSAGE:

USE THIS AFFIRMATION: I AM GUIDED AND BLESSED WITH THE CROW'S ENERGY AND AM READY TO RECEIVE EVERYTHING THAT IS COMING TO ME

EMBRACE THE CROWS BLESSING TO WELCOME YOU INTO THE COSMOS.

"The Crow's Blessing" message within the Crow Oracle bestows a profound sentiment of protection, guidance, and good fortune, drawing inspiration from the crow's storied role as a bridge between different realms of existence.

Crows, with their ethereal allure and presence across myriad cultures, are often regarded as protectors and guides for souls navigating the liminal spaces between the living and the spiritual. "The Crow's Blessing" speaks to this time-honored belief, extending a wish that the crow's blessings accompany one on their own metaphysical journey.

This message serves as a reminder that, as we traverse the myriad phases and realms of our lives, be they physical, emotional, or spiritual, we are never truly alone. The crow, as an emblem of spiritual guidance, watches over us, offering protection and wisdom. Its blessing is an assurance of safe passage and enlightenment.

"The Crow's Blessing" also carries with it an invitation: to open oneself to the universe, to trust in the wisdom of ancient spirits like the crow, and to recognize that our journey through life's realms is a sacred pilgrimage, imbued with hidden lessons and cosmic significance.

Furthermore, this message instills a sense of reverence for the crow as a guardian and guide. In seeking its blessings, one also acknowledges the crow's role in the grand tapestry of existence, cherishing its timeless wisdom and protective presence.

"The Crow's Blessing" extends a heartfelt wish for protection, guidance, and enlightenment as one navigates the intricate dance between realms of existence. It underscores the crow's cherished role as a protector and guide, encouraging us to embrace our journey with trust, reverence, and the assurance that the blessings of ancient spirits like the crow accompany us every step of the way.

45
THE CLOSING OF THE CIRCLE

CLOSING IS NOT THE END, BUT THE BEGINNING OF SOMETHING NEW

MESSAGE:

AS THE CROW RETURNS TO THE UNSEEN REALMS, REMEMBER THAT THE CIRCLE IS NEVER TRULY BROKEN.

ALLOW FOR NEW DOORS TO OPEN WHEN IT IS TIME CLOSE ANOTHER.

"The Closing of the Circle" message within the Crow Oracle imparts a profound lesson about the cyclical nature of existence, the continuity of life's journey, and the idea that even as the crow returns to the unseen realms, the circle of life is never truly broken.

Crows, with their symbolic role as messengers between realms and their associations with cycles and transformation, embody the concept of the eternal and unending journey. "The Closing of the Circle" encourages us to recognize that life's journey is not linear but cyclical, much like the flight patterns of the crow.

This message prompts us to embrace the idea that, even in moments of transition, loss, or change, there is a sense of continuity. The crow's return to the unseen realms serves as a reminder that, although life takes different forms and phases, it is all part of a larger cosmic cycle.

"The Closing of the Circle" suggests that closure and endings are not finality but transitions to new beginnings. It encourages us to see the beauty in the interconnections of all things and the constant renewal of life's energies.

Furthermore, this message underscores the idea that the circle of life is a source of wisdom and comfort. Just as the crow's flight patterns return it to its origins, our own journeys bring us back to our essential selves, enriched by the experiences and lessons along the way.

"The Closing of the Circle" inspires us to embrace the cyclical nature of life's journey, much like the crow's return to the unseen realms. It encourages us to see transitions and endings as part of a larger cosmic cycle, where each phase enriches the next. By recognizing the continuity of existence, we can navigate life with a sense of acceptance, resilience, and a deeper understanding of the unbroken circle that binds all things in the grand tapestry of the universe.

46
THE CROW'S FAREWELL

HONOR THOSE MOMENTS IN YOUR LIFE WHEN THE CROW APPEARS

MESSAGE:

BID FAREWELL TO THE CROW WITH GRATITUDE, FOR THEIR MESSAGES WILL FOREVER GUIDE YOU.

EMBRACE THE BEAUTY OF PRECISE MOMENTS IN YOUR LIFE.

"The Crow's Farewell" message within the Crow Oracle imparts a bittersweet but profound lesson about the transitory nature of physical presence and the enduring influence of wisdom and guidance.

Crows, as messengers and symbols of wisdom, often make fleeting appearances in our lives, and their physical presence is temporary. "The Crow's Farewell" reminds us that, like all physical beings, the crow eventually departs from our immediate surroundings.

This message prompts us to embrace the impermanence of life and to appreciate the beauty of moments when the crow graces us with its presence. It encourages us to recognize that even though the crow may physically depart, its messages and guidance remain with us as enduring gifts.

"The Crow's Farewell" suggests that gratitude is a fitting response when the crow departs. Gratitude for the wisdom and insights it has shared, and for the reminders to be attentive to the mysteries of existence.

Furthermore, this message underscores the idea that the crow's departure is not a farewell in the truest sense but a transition to a different form of presence. The lessons and messages it has conveyed continue to guide us, offering wisdom and insight long after its physical presence has faded.

In summary, "The Crow's Farewell" inspires us to bid farewell to the crow with gratitude, recognizing that its messages and guidance are enduring gifts that continue to guide us. It encourages us to embrace the impermanence of physical presence while cherishing the wisdom and insights that remain with us as lasting companions on our life's journey.

47
ACKNOWLEDGMENTS

CHERISH THE INNER GUIDANCE YOU HAVE GAINED FROM THE CROW

MESSAGE:

BID FAREWELL TO THE CROW WITH GRATITUDE, FOR THEIR MESSAGES WILL FOREVER GUIDE YOU.

NAVIGATING THE ABYSS WITHIN

The "Acknowledgments" message within the Crow Oracle encapsulates a fundamental and beautiful aspect of our spiritual journey: gratitude. It serves as a reminder of the importance of recognizing and appreciating the wisdom and messages we receive from the crow, this enigmatic messenger between worlds.

Crows, with their symbolism as bearers of wisdom and conduits to the mystical, invite us to acknowledge the profound lessons they impart. The "Acknowledgments" message prompts us to take a moment to pause and express our heartfelt gratitude for the crow's presence in our lives.

This message encourages us to be mindful of the blessings that come with the crow's wisdom. It reminds us that gratitude is a transformative practice, allowing us to deepen our connection to the messages and lessons offered by the crow, and to the spiritual realms beyond.

Furthermore, the message underscores the idea that gratitude is a form of reciprocity. Just as the crow shares its wisdom with us, our acknowledgment and gratitude are a way of reciprocating, honoring the sacred exchange between the earthly and the divine.

In summary, the "Acknowledgments" message inspires us to express gratitude for the crow's wisdom and the messages they bring from beyond realms. It encourages us to recognize the profound impact of these teachings on our spiritual journey and to reciprocate the blessings we receive with an open heart and deep appreciation. Through gratitude, we deepen our connection to the crow's messages and to the spiritual dimensions they represent.

48

COMPLETION

COMPLETION MEANS YOU HAVE WORKED HARD TO ENDURE, MAINTAIN AND ACCEPT SITUATIONS

MESSAGE:

YOUR JOURNEY WITH THE CROW IS COMPLETE. MAY ITS WISDOM GUIDE YOU ALWAYS.

BE CONFIDENT THAT YOU HAVE ALL THE SUPPORT FROM THE CROW'S ENERGY TO COMPLETE ANYTHING IN YOUR LIFE.

The "Completion" message within the Crow's energy brings a sense of closure and reflection to the journey we've undertaken with the crow as our guide. It signifies the end of a chapter, but it also carries the essence of continuity and a profound wish for enduring wisdom.

As we conclude our journey with the Crow's Oracle, we are reminded of the cyclical nature of life's experiences, much like the flight patterns of the crow. This message encourages us to acknowledge the completeness of our current phase, understanding that every ending is the beginning of a new chapter.

"The Completion" message prompts us to reflect upon the lessons we've learned and the insights we've gained through our interactions with the crow. It signifies a moment of transition, much like the crow's own return to the unseen realms, where we take the wisdom we've acquired into the next phase of our journey.

Furthermore, this message underscores the idea that the wisdom we've received from the Crow's Oracle is not confined to a single moment in time but serves as an enduring source of guidance. The crow's teachings remain with us as timeless wisdom, always available to provide insight and clarity on our path.

"Completion" message is a heartfelt acknowledgment of the journey we've taken with the Crow's Oracle. It signifies both an ending and a beginning, encouraging us to carry the wisdom gained with us as we continue our life's journey. Through reflection and integration, we can navigate life with a profound sense of completeness, knowing that the crow's wisdom will guide us always.

CONCLUSION

In the final pages of the Crow's Oracle, we find ourselves at the threshold of a profound journey, an exploration into the mystical realm where the crow reigns as a symbol of wisdom, a messenger of hidden truths, and an unwavering guide between the worlds. As we reflect on the wisdom imparted within these 48 pages, we are reminded of the timeless significance that this enigmatic bird holds in the vast tapestry of human spirituality.

The crow, revered across diverse cultures and epochs, invites us to transcend the boundaries of the ordinary and embrace the extraordinary.

With each message unveiled in this oracle, we are beckoned to look beyond the mundane, to seek a deeper connection with the cosmic, and to recognize the eternal dance between the seen and the unseen.

These pages are a repository of sacred keys, each message a doorway to the profound wisdom residing within our own souls. As we turn the pages, we discover inspiration, clarity, and insight, providing us with the tools to navigate the intricate labyrinth of our life's journey.

The crow's messages, timeless echoes from ages past, bridge the chasm between practicality and mysticism. They offer us guidance and solace, reminding us that our existence is a dance between the ordinary and the extraordinary, the known and the unknown.

Within this oracle, you are not alone. The crow, your eternal companion, will accompany you every step of the way. Its wisdom will be your beacon in the darkest hours, your compass in uncharted territory, and your confidant in moments of uncertainty.

May this oracle book be a wellspring of inspiration, a mirror for reflection, and a source of empowerment. As you journey through its pages, may you embrace the winds of change, discover the clarity you seek, and awaken the inner wisdom that has slumbered within you. Welcome to the mystical world of the Crow's Oracle, where the crow's caw reverberates across dimensions, guiding you to the profound truths that lie both within and beyond.

ABOUT THE AUTHORS

Rudi De Ponte and Dimitri Kalogeropoulos are two remarkable souls who have united their unique gifts and divine intuitions to inspire, heal, and elevate humanity through their profound spiritual journey.

Their collaborative efforts have birthed a synergy that bridges the realms of healing, well-being, and spiritual enlightenment. With a shared vision to create a world of pure beings living in peace, love, and harmony, Rudi and Dimitri have become beacons of light, guiding others on their paths of self-discovery and transformation.

Rudi De Ponte is a luminous presence in the realm of healing and spiritual connection. With an innate ability to tap into the universal energies and receive direct insights from the source, Rudi has become a conduit for divine downloads that offer guidance, healing, and deep transformation. Through years of dedicated practice and attunement to the rhythms of the cosmos, Rudi has developed a unique approach to healing that resonates with the very essence of the universe. His intuitive gifts have helped countless individuals navigate through their challenges, facilitating profound shifts on emotional, physical, and spiritual levels.

On the other hand, Dimitri Kalogeropoulos brings his wisdom and focus to the arena of holistic well-being. With an emphasis on nourishing the body, mind, and spirit, he advocates for the integration of mindful eating, conscious movement, and spiritual alignment with breathwork and meditation. His journey has led him to master the art of balance, and his teachings reflect his deep understanding of the interconnectedness of these elements in fostering overall vitality and harmony. His insights empower individuals to cultivate self-love, make conscious choices, and embark on a transformative journey toward holistic well-being.

Together, Rudi and Dimitri create a harmonious symphony that blends intuitive healing with holistic well-being, guiding readers toward an integrated approach to self-discovery and personal growth.

Their books are not mere intellectual offerings; they are divinely guided manifestations of their lived experiences, spiritual revelations, and practical insights. Every word penned by this dynamic duo is a testament to their unwavering commitment to spreading love, light, and wisdom to the world.

Rudi and Dimitri's mission is clear: to touch hearts and awaken souls. Through their collaborative works, they illuminate the path to self-realization, inviting readers to embark on a transformative journey that leads to the awakening of their true potential. As souls united by a shared purpose, Rudi De Ponte and Dimitri Kalogeropoulos inspire us to embrace our innate divinity, cultivate inner peace, radiate love, and contribute to the collective evolution of consciousness.

Their books are more than literary creations; they are powerful tools for personal and planetary transformation. By opening these pages, you embark on a journey guided by the wisdom of two souls who have dedicated their lives to channeling the energies of the universe and spirit, offering us a blueprint for creating a world of pure beings existing in harmony and love.

NOTES

NOTES

NOTES

NOTES

Printed in Great Britain
by Amazon